Measuring Migration Conference 2022
Conference Proceedings

Measuring Migration Conference 2022

Conference Proceedings

Compiled by
Christina Pao and Maksim Zubok

Sponsored by MigrationOxford and Nuffield College at the
University of Oxford

This publication was made open access by the Princeton University Library Open Access Fund.

TRANSNATIONAL PRESS LONDON
2022

Migration Series: 42

Measuring Migration Conference 2022 Conference Proceedings

Compiled by Christina Pao and Maksim Zubok

First published in 2022 by TRANSNATIONAL PRESS LONDON in the United Kingdom, 13 Stamford Place, Sale, M33 3BT, UK.
www.tplondon.com

Transnational Press London® and the logo and its affiliated brands are registered trademarks.

Requests for permission to reproduce material from this work should be sent to:
admin@tplondon.com

Paperback
ISBN: 978-1-80135-180-5
Digital
ISBN: 978-1-80135-181-2

Cover Design: Nihal Yazgan

Transnational Press London Ltd. is a company registered in England and Wales No. 8771684

CONTENTS

MEASURING MIGRATION CONFERENCE 2022

The conference, "Measuring Migration: How? When? Why?", was an interdisciplinary and international venue for academics, practitioners, and students to explore the idea of "measuring" migration" using a variety of methods from interdisciplinary perspectives. Participants explored the ethics and implications of what it means to track migratory flows and discussed when this might be appropriate and why these data are helpful/harmful.

This conference was hosted in hybrid format online and in-person at the University of Oxford on June 9-10, 2022 (Oxford, England, UK) and was sponsored by MigrationOxford (previously known as the Migration and Mobility Network) and Nuffield College. There were over 300 participants registered from around the world, spanning six continents and dozens of institutions. There were over 30 paper presentations on 10 panels and four keynote addresses/panels that took place over the two days. The proceedings included in this volume cover the majority of the papers presented.

We would like to thank our colleagues who served on the program and steering committees, as well as those who helped us on the ground as local coordinators. We are particularly grateful for our funders at Nuffield College and MigrationOxford for their faith in the success of this event. Most of all, we would like to thank our speakers and presenters who came in-person and online to participate in the first Measuring Migration conference in this series.

Organisers	Christina Pao (Nuffield College, University of Oxford)
	Maksim Zubok (Nuffield College, University of Oxford)
Steering Committee	Domiziana Turcatti (MMN, COMPAS, University of Oxford)
	Jacqueline Broadhead (COMPAS, University of Oxford)
Local Coordinators	Hera Jay Brown (ODID, University of Oxford)
	Sarena Martinez (Dept. of History, University of Oxford)
Program Committee	Gilda Borriello (COMPAS, University of Oxford)
	Hera Jay Brown (ODID, University of Oxford)
	Yinglei Chen (COMPAS, University of Oxford)
	Scarlett Ng (Dept. of Sociology, University of Oxford)
	Daisy Pollenne (COMPAS, University of Oxford)
	Francesco Rampazzo (Nuffield College, University of Oxford)
	Marwan Safar Jalani (DPIR, University of Oxford)

Further Thanks To... (in no particular order): Giuliana Forestieri (Nuffield Conference Director); Olivier Goddet and All Catering Staff (Nuffield Buttery/Catering); Karen Richardson, Mark Norman, Salman Pasha, and Matthew Lake (Nuffield IT); Nathan Grassi (COMPAS Administrator); Sarah Milne Das, Eleni Kechagia-Ovseiko, Justine Crump and the Nuffield Academic Office; Peter Marshall and the Nuffield Finance Department; Catherine Farfan, Monica Esposito-West, and the Nuffield Development Office; Claire Bunce (Nuffield Bursary Office); The Nuffield Lodge; The Nuffield Scouts; The Members of the Nuffield GCC.

ORGANIZERS' WELCOME

We are absolutely delighted to welcome participants across many different disciplines, focus areas, experiences, and different professional backgrounds including in the academy, nonprofits, intergovernmental agencies, and activist organizations. We hope you will foster connections that will go beyond our two-day conference and discover new perspectives, topics, approaches in migration research.

In organizing the conference, we wanted to critically reflect on the research and practice of measuring migration. To what extent is it possible to make methodologically sound, "valid" measurement of migratory flows? What data and methods are used to derive these measurements, and what harms can data acquisition inflict on people? How does research inform policymaking, and what are broader impacts of performing migration research on the lives of people, for better or for worse?

These questions are particularly relevant in light of the many facets of social change. The COVID-19 pandemic has, for many, changed the means of and reasons for migration, and the pandemic has also changed the way researchers have had to collect migration data. Further, advances in fields, such as digital demography, have changed the methods that are used to analyse and visualize data. Digitalization brings forward large volumes of data that enable researchers to tackle questions previously thought to be infeasible to work on.

With these burgeoning methods and data, there are increased concerns about data protection and privacy: For example, there are manifold implications for ethics around the use of digital trace data and AI. This conference hopes to bridge these ideas—changing social realities, advances in data and methods, and need for ethical approaches—across different branches of migration research.

Maksim Zubok and Christina Pao

Conference Organizers

PROGRAMME

June 9th, 2022

10am-11:15am Opening Keynote **(Nikola Sander)**

11:30am-1pm Parallel Sessions 1

How do we measure migration? Methods and advancements **(Discussant: Francesco Rampazzo)**

When should we qualify and not quantify? Data and theory **(Discussant: Funda Ustek Spilda)**

1pm-2:30pm Lunch Talk: Survey methods and migration—Benefits and challenges **(Isabel Ruiz and Mariña Fernández-Reino)**

2:30-4pm Parallel Sessions 2

When should we measure migration? Ethical considerations of data collection and harm mitigation **(Discussant: Matthew Gibney)**

What are migration data? Past and present data and their challenges **(Discussant: Anna Krausova)**

4:30pm-6pm Parallel Sessions 3

What are the implications of measuring migration? Policies and interventions **(Discussant: Madeleine Sumption)**

What are the implications of measuring migration? Frameworks, data, and theory **(Discussant: Marie Mallet-Garcia)**

June 10th, 2022

10:30am-12pm Parallel Sessions 4

How do we represent migration? Developments in data visualization **(Discussant: William Allen)**

How do we represent migration? The impacts of space and geography **(Discussant: Dora Sampaio)**

12pm-1:30pm Lunch Talk: Migration and the Potentials of Digital Trace Data **(Ridhi Kashyap and Francesco Rampazzo)**

1:30pm-3pm Parallel Sessions 5

How has COVID-19 affected migration and mobility? Capturing changing patterns **(Discussant: Ram Babu Bhagat)**

How has COVID-19 affected methods for migration scholars? Crisis and measurement **(Discussant: Irene Schöfberger)**

3:45pm-5:45pm Closing Panel: Migration measurement at a crossroads **(Olivier Sterck, Mina Fazel, and Carlos Vargas Silva)**

MIGRATION NETWORKS: AN APPLICATION FOR MEASURING MIGRATION

Ivette Contreras-Gonzalez[1]

Introduction

Former immigrants are widely believed to pave the way for new immigrants and to influence their life decisions in host countries. The groups of immigrants are usually called immigrants enclaves or networks. These networks play several roles, such as reducing migration costs and uncertainty. Previous research finds that networks' members can provide referrals so that new migrants can get new jobs easily (Munshi, 2003).

However, the lack of data of migration including the origin and destination of migrants has been a handicap for the estimation of networks effects. This paper uses as an example the networks formed by Salvadoran immigrants in the U.S., and it contributes to the literature by proposing the use of administrative data that can be exploited to understand the interconnectedness of migrants' networks. Exploring new data sources that can shed light on the origin and destination of immigrants may help to better understand the causes that lie behind the decision of migrating. A further application using this dataset can be found in Contreras (2022) which estimates the effect of the network size on education decisions of young Salvadoran immigrants.

Background of Salvadoran emigration to the U.S.

This section provides a brief description of the Salvadoran emigration to the U.S. Three out of ten Salvadorans live in the United States (Ruggles, et al., 2021), with remittances representing more than 20% of El Salvador's GDP in the last 25 years (BCR, 2020). Before 1980, the Salvadoran migration to the U.S. was small, according to the Migration Policy Institute (2007). The number of Salvadoran immigrants exploded during 1980 while a civil war increased violence levels within the country (De la Cruz, 2017).

Table 1 shows the total number of the foreign-born population who live in the U.S. and the number of the Salvadoran foreign-born population (SFB) in the U.S. across different years. The number of Salvadoran immigrants increased from 15,717 in 1970 to 465,433 in 1990, approximately 30 times the population estimated in 1970 (see Table 1). The average annual growth of the SFB in the U.S. during the 1980s was 50.1%.

---

[1] I gratefully acknowledge the DGM (Salvadoran General Office of Migration) for giving access to the dataset used in this paper. I thank Paul Carrillo (GWU), Bryan Stuart (Federal Reserve Bank of Philadelphia), Marisol Rodriguez Chatruc (IDB), and Michael Clemens (CGDev) for their helpful comments and suggestions, as well as conference participants at the SITE conference on immigration at Stanford in 2019. All errors are my own.

Table 1. Foreign-born populations in the U.S.

| year | Foreign-born population (any country) | Salvadoran foreign-born population | | Rank[2] | Average annual growth |
		Number	Share of all foreign-born		
1960	9,738,091	6,310	0.06%	54	
1970	9,619,302	15,717	0.16%	53	14.90%
1980	14,079,906	94,447	0.67%	28	50.10%
1990	19,797,316	465,433	2.35%	11	39.30%
2000	31,107,889	817,336	2.63%	9	7.60%
2008	37,960,773	1,094,993	2.88%	6	4.20%
2016	43,738,901	1,387,022	3.17%	6	3.30%

Source: Data for 2016 from the American Community Survey 2016.
Note: Data for earlier years from Migration Policy Institute based on Census data and American Community Survey 2008, and 2016.

Even though the civil war ended in 1992 and the growth of emigration flows decreased, emigration still plays a relevant role in the Salvadoran economy. In the last 10 years, 9.5 percent of all the apprehensions in the U.S. Southwest Border include Salvadoran citizens (on average, 43,894 apprehensions per year). In the same period, 15.6 percent of the apprehensions of unaccompanied children included Salvadoran citizens (U.S. Customs and Border Protection, 2022).

Data

This section explores the dataset used to understand the interconnectedness of Salvadoran immigrants in the U.S. with their municipalities of origin. It includes information about the municipality of origin in El Salvador and the U.S. County of destination of the Salvadoran-born population who renewed or obtained a Salvadoran passport in the U.S. between 2000 to 2016. For each observation, the municipality of origin (in El Salvador) and the county of destination (in the U.S) is included, as well as information on birthdate and sex. This dataset was created by the General Office of Migration (DGM) in El Salvador.

According to the U.S. Department of Homeland Security (2021), El Salvador is the second leading source of unauthorized immigration to the U.S. Approximately, 1 out of 2 Salvadorans in the U.S. is classified as an unauthorized immigrant (Department of Homeland Security, 2021). Consequently, they do not have any U.S. identification document. However, they can get a Salvadoran passport (or renew their own) at a Salvadoran Embassy or Consulate. Having a valid passport allows them at least to send money back home and it serves as an identification for their life in the U.S. Then, it is expected that most of Salvadoran immigrants renew their passports while they are in the U.S.

The DGM dataset shows that the settlement patterns from different provinces of El Salvador to states in the U.S. are not homogenous. Figures 1 and 2 show the distribution of the Salvadoran immigrants in the U.S. by region of origin and State in the destination. Different states have populations from different Salvadoran provinces. For example, California has populations from San Salvador and Santa Ana, while Maryland's main source of SFBs are La Unión and San Miguel, and New York has more SFBs from La Unión and Morazán. The heterogeneity of the settlement patterns may show that previous migrants have a role on the decision of emigrating and also on the decision of where to settle after arriving to the U.S.

---

[2] The column "Rank" shows the position of the Salvadoran foreign-born population in the total foreign-born population.

Another contribution of this type of data is capturing the place of origin of immigrants. In general, migration statistics that aim to collect data on migrants (at the origin) use household surveys or censuses where households report if a member has emigrated. However, this approach does not include the households that have emigrated as a whole. In that sense, data that connects the origin and destination of migrants can help to avoid the selection bias created by surveys/censuses at the place of origin or destination.

Figure 1. Settlement patterns of Salvadoran immigrants in the U.S.

Source: Own elaboration based on DGM database (2016)
Note: This figure shows the distribution of Salvadoran foreign-born population (SFB) living in the U.S. classified by their sending regions in El Salvador and their destination regions in the U.S.

Figure 2. Settlement patterns of Salvadoran immigrants in the U.S.

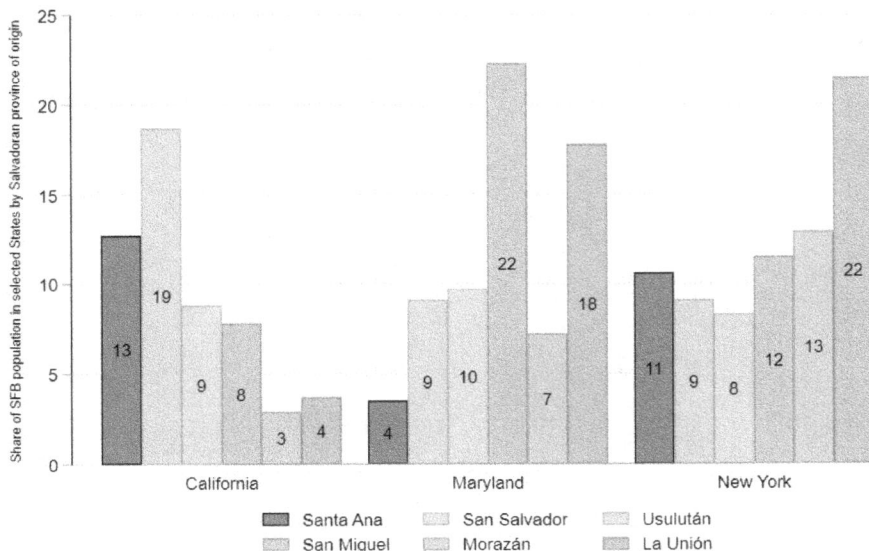

Source: Own elaboration based on DGM database (2016)

Data validation of the DGM database

A question that may be raised is if this dataset shows a similar distribution of Salvadoran migrants in surveys conducted in the U.S. and in El Salvador. To address this issue, Figure 3 shows the correlation between the pooled DGM dataset and the American Community Survey 2016 (Ruggles et al., 2021). The figure shows the number of Salvadoran immigrants in the U.S. as a share of the population by State (in logarithmic scale) in both datasets. After running a simple linear regression that correlates this indicator in the DGM dataset with the same in the ACS 2016, I find an r-squared of 0.88. In other words, both results are highly correlated, which provides evidence to the hypothesis that the DGM dataset is consistent with existing data.

Furthermore, I compare the DGM dataset with the last population Census in El Salvador, which was conducted in 2007. Each household had to answer how many household members were living abroad. For each of them, the country where they lived was recorded. I keep the household members that live in the U.S. Then, I estimate the number of Salvadoran-born living in the U.S. reported in the Census by municipality. Finally, I calculate the share of Salvadoran-born reported with respect to the population in the municipality.

Figure 3. Relationship between DGM dataset and ACS (2016)

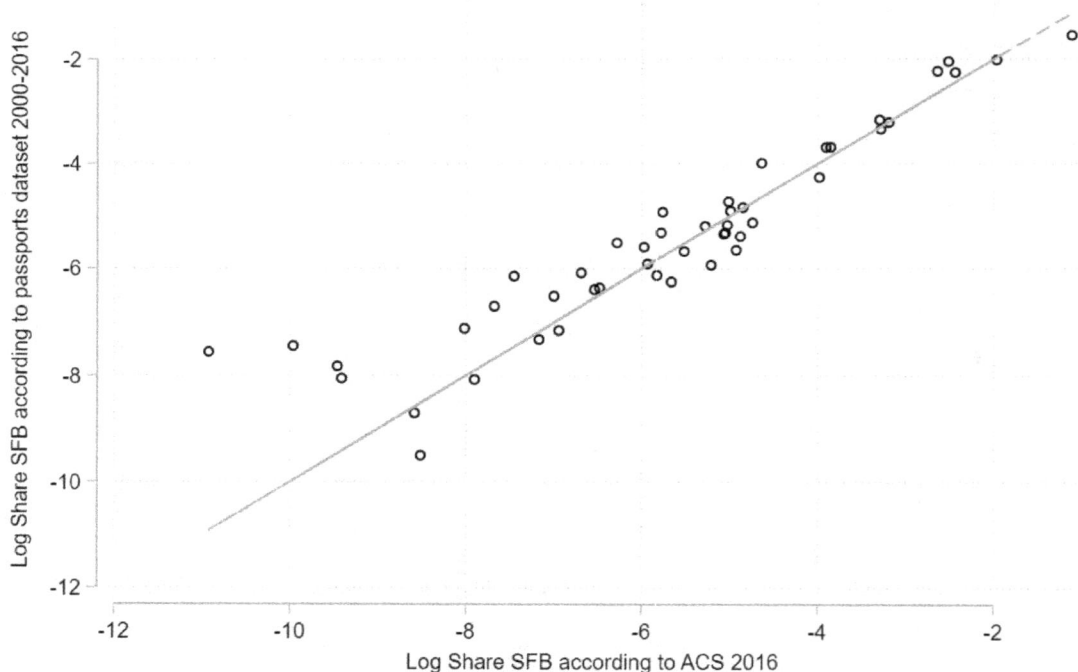

In addition, I pool the DGM dataset from 2000 to 2007, and calculate the number of Salvadoran-born population reported in this dataset. Then I estimate the share of Salvadoran-born with respect to the population in the municipality. The logged results are presented in Figure 4, as in the previous analysis, I run a simple regression that correlates both indicators and we found an r-squared of 0.70. In other words, both indicators are highly correlated.

Why is the correlation between the DGM dataset (2000-2007) and the population Salvadoran Census 2007 lower than the one estimated when comparing the DGM dataset (2000-2016) with ACS 2016? The main reason that may explain this difference is that some households emigrated with all their members, therefore they are not accounted in the Salvadoran Census. Even though, the correlation is high and provides evidence of the DGM dataset's alignment with existing data; it is important to point out that this descriptive analysis has its own limitations since it does not provide causal estimates. Further research can explore how this type of data is correlated with other surveys in different periods.

Figure 4. Salvadoran Passports dataset 2000-2008 with Salvadoran Census 2007

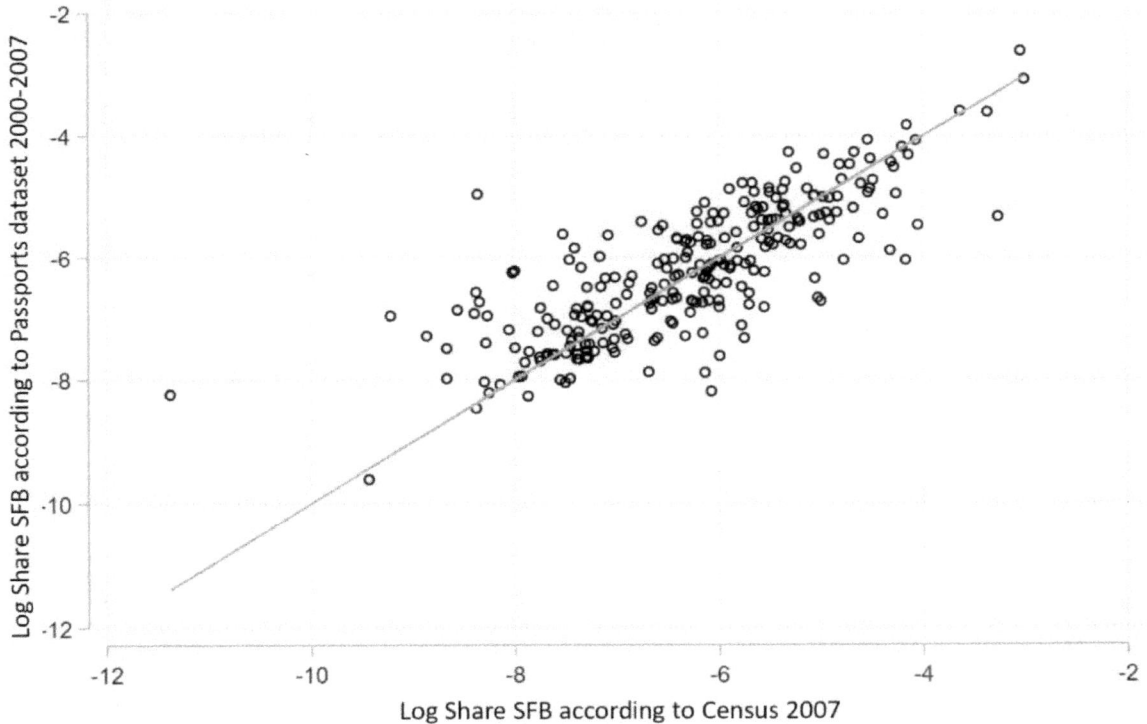

Source: Own elaboration based on DGM (2017) and DIGESTYC (2008)

Note: For this figure, I compare the DGM dataset with the last population Census in El Salvador, which was conducted in 2007. I calculate the share of Salvadoran-born reported with respect to the population in the municipality. For the DGM dataset, I pool the data from 2000 to 2007 and calculate the number of Salvadoran-born with respect to the population in the municipality. The logged results are presented in this figure.

Conclusions

This short paper discusses how an anonymized passports dataset can help to understand the interconnectedness of the Salvadoran migrants in the U.S. I provide evidence that the number of migrants estimated using the DGM dataset is highly correlated with similar statistics created using the

American Community Survey 2016 and the last Salvadoran population Census conducted in 2007. A further application using this dataset can be found in Contreras (2022) which estimates the effect of the network size on education decisions of young Salvadoran immigrants.

More research on the consequences of measuring migration is also needed. Even though administrative data can provide insights on the interconnectedness between places of origin and destination, data protocols are needed to ensure anonymization and prevent any harm to the migrant population.

References

BCR. (2020). *Base de datos económica y financiera de El Salvador.*

Contreras, I. (2022). *Following your Lead: Migration Networks and Immigrants' Education Decisions.* Unpublished manuscript.

De la Cruz, R. (2017). No Asylum for the Innocent: Gendered Representations of Salvadoran Refugees in the 1980s. The American Behavioral Scientist, 1103-1118.

Department of Homeland Security. (2021). *Estimates of the Unauthorized Immigrant Population Residing in the United States: January 2021.*

Migration Policy Institute. (2007). *El Salvador despite end to civil war, emigration continues.*

Munshi, K. (2003). Networks in the Modern Economy: Mexican Migrants in the U.S. The Quarterly Journal of Economics, 549-599.

Patel, K., & Vella, F. (2013). Immigrant Networks and Their Implications for Occupational Choice and Wages. The Review of Economics and Statistics, 1249-1277.

Ruggles, S., Flood, S., Foster, S., Goeken, R., Pacas, J., Schouweiler, M., & Sobek, M. (2021). IPUMS USA. Dataset.

U.S. Customs and Border Protection. (2022, August 15). Southwest Land Border Encounters. Retrieved from https://www.cbp.gov/newsroom/stats/southwest-land-border-encounters

USE OF NON-TRADITIONAL DATA SOURCES TO NOWCAST MIGRATION TRENDS THROUGH ARTIFICIAL INTELLIGENCE TECHNOLOGIES

Diletta Goglia[1,2], Laura Pollacci[1], and Alina Sîrbu[1]

Background and motivation

In recent years the pursuit of original drivers and methods is becoming an increasing requirement for migration studies, considering the new technologies used to characterise and understand the human migration phenomenon. In addition to the traditional data typically used in migration studies (e.g., indicators related to the labour market or economic status, measures obtained from surveys and official statistics, either from national censuses or from the population registries), many researchers like Bosco et al. (2022), Fiorio et al. (2017), Gendronneau et al. (2019), Jisu, Sîrbu, Rossetti, Giannotti, and Rapoport (2021), Salah (2021), Spyratos et al. (2018), Sîrbu et al. (2021), Zagheni, Garimella, Weber, and State (2014), Zagheni, Polimis, Alexander, Weber, and Billari (2018), Zagheni, Weber, and Gummadi (2017), have proposed to employ non-traditional data sources to study migration. These can consist in news data, satellite data, but also in digital traces of humans generated by using internet services, mobile phones, IoT devices, fidelity cards, online social networks and many others. This unconventional approach is intended to find an alternative methodology to answer open questions about the human migration framework (i.e., nowcasting flows and stocks, studying the integration of multiple sources and knowledge, and investigating migration drivers). The new data have the advantage of timeliness and large geographical coverage, but also disadvantages in terms of selection bias and amount of resources required to process, as reported by Sîrbu et al. (2021) and Pollacci, Milli, Bircan, and Rossetti (2022). Therefore, models extracted from these data need to be carefully validated, typically with traditional data sources. In this context of meaningful data combination, many types of data exist, still very scattered and heterogeneous, making integration far from straightforward.

Contributions

Our work focuses on the integrated use of heterogeneous traditional datasets and new data types. We propose two different contributions: MIMI, a new multi-feature dataset presented in Goglia (2022) and Goglia, Pollacci, and Sîrbu (2022), and a new regression analysis that could significantly contribute to the study of migration drivers and, in future work, to forecast emerging trends through the use of Artificial Intelligence technologies.

The MIMI dataset

The Multi-aspect Integrated Migration Indicators (MIMI) dataset is intended to be exploited in

[1] Department of Computer Science, University of Pisa, Pisa, Italy. E-mail: d.goglia@studenti.unipi.it

[2] This work is supported by the European Union – Horizon 2020 Program under the scheme "INFRAIA-01-2018-2019 – Integrating Activities for Advanced Communities", Grant Agreement n.871042, "SoBigData++: European Integrated Infrastructure for Social Mining and Big Data Analytics", and by the Horizon2020. European project "HumMingBird – Enhanced migration measures from a multidimensional perspective", Grant Agreement n. 870661.

15

migration studies and is a concrete example of integration of traditional and non-traditional data sources. It includes official data about bidirectional human migration (traditional country-to-country flow and stock data, retrieved from EUROSTAT and United Nations public datasets), multidisciplinary variables and original indicators, including economic, demographic, cultural and geographic indicators, together with the Facebook Social Connectedness Index (SCI) released by Meta (2021). The dataset was released under the Creative Commons Attribution 4.0 International Public License (CC BY 4.0) and is publicly available on Zenodo at the following link: https://doi.org/10.5281/zenodo.6493325. It contains more than 28,000 records and 870 different variables and covers 255 different countries, identified by ISO-3166 standard notation.

The integration process uniformised the data coming from various sources, in an attempt to fill in gaps and missing data, standardise location and time dimensions, and ultimately facilitate use by the research community. Thanks to this variety of knowledge, experts from several research fields (demographers, sociologists, economists) could exploit MIMI to investigate the trends in the various indicators, and the relationship among them. Moreover, it could be possible to develop complex models based on this dataset to assess human migration by evaluating related interdisciplinary drivers, and to nowcast/predict traditional migration indicators through non-traditional variables, such as the strength of social connectivity. Here, the Facebook SCI could have an important role. It guarantees an anonymised collection of information on users and their friendships, measuring the relative probability that two individuals across two countries are friends on Facebook. Therefore, it could be employed as a proxy of social connections across borders to be studied as a possible driver of migration.

As example of salient patterns observed among various indicators included in the MIMI dataset, Figure 1 shows correlations between migration flows and Facebook SCI using the Spearman and Kendall coefficients. P-values have been computed in order to confirm of refute the relevance of each correlation value: results are indicated in heatmaps with a number of asterisks proportional to the relevance obtained:

no asterisks	no relevance	$p\text{-value} \geq 0.05$
*	moderate relevance	$0.01 \leq p\text{-value} < 0.05$
**	high relevance	$0.001 \leq p\text{-value} < 0.01$
***	very high relevance	$p\text{-value} < 0.001$

We observe significant positive correlation between migration flows and SCI, indicating that social connectedness may be an important migration driver, and that SCI could be employed to estimate migration flows.

Figure 1. Kendall's tau-b and Spearman rank-order correlations between SCI and migration flows by citizenship and by residence for both UN and EUROSTAT sources. Measures of Facebook SCI are available in the MIMI dataset for both 2020 and 2021. They have been correlated with the most recent data available for migration flows, i.e., 2019.

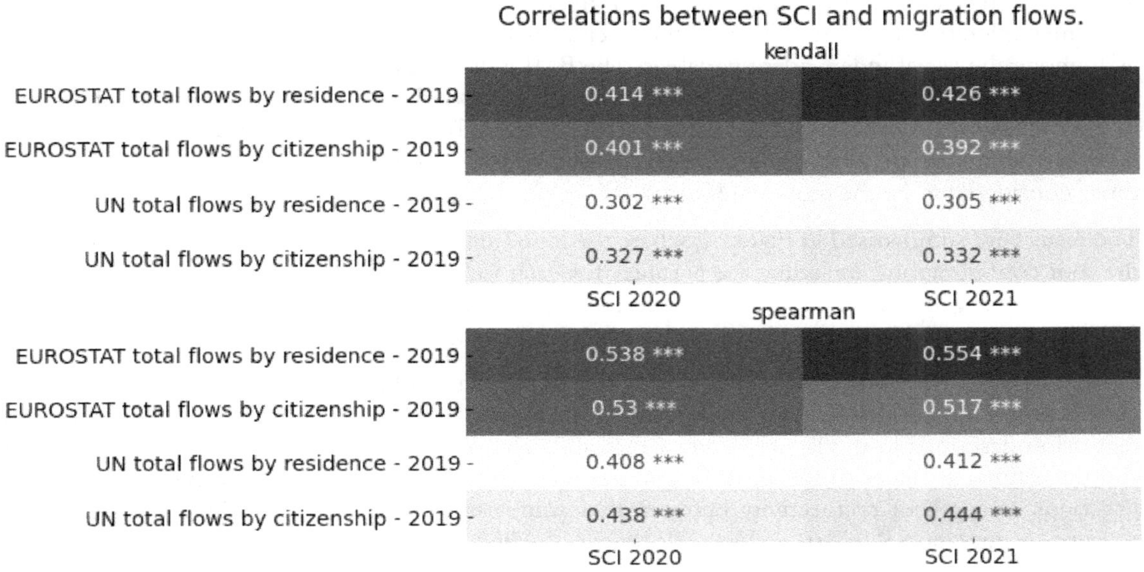

Correlations between SCI and migration flows.

kendall

	SCI 2020	SCI 2021
EUROSTAT total flows by residence - 2019	0.414 ***	0.426 ***
EUROSTAT total flows by citizenship - 2019	0.401 ***	0.392 ***
UN total flows by residence - 2019	0.302 ***	0.305 ***
UN total flows by citizenship - 2019	0.327 ***	0.332 ***

spearman

	SCI 2020	SCI 2021
EUROSTAT total flows by residence - 2019	0.538 ***	0.554 ***
EUROSTAT total flows by citizenship - 2019	0.53 ***	0.517 ***
UN total flows by residence - 2019	0.408 ***	0.412 ***
UN total flows by citizenship - 2019	0.438 ***	0.444 ***

Migration drivers

Our second contribution is an analysis of the relation between indicators included in the MIMI dataset, through regression analysis. We present a new measure, the Bidirectional Migration Index (BMI) indicator, which takes into account both the inflows and outflows shared by two countries i and j, and which is defined for each year t as follows:

$$BMI(t) = \frac{Flow_{i \to j}(t) + Flow_{j \to i}(t)}{Pop_i(t) \cdot Pop_j(t)}$$

We predict the values of the BMI starting from SCI and other indicators through an ordinary least squares statistical model (OLS) that performs a linear regression to estimate migration trends in order to understand which variables, among those included in the MIMI dataset, are related to the flows and therefore could be considered migration drivers. At this stage, our goal is to understand which factors are significant for the purpose of predicting migration. Specifically, the OLS model fits a subset of variables derived from the MIMI dataset and related to each country pair i and j, and evaluates their relevance for estimating the BMI. Besides Facebook SCI, we include:

- as numerical variables: the distance between the two countries, difference and mean GDP (related to 2018, as the nearest available year with respect to the SCI reference period), area, number and percentage of Facebook users of the two countries, difference between each cultural indicator of the two countries;

- as binarized categorical variables: indicators that express whether the two countries share border, religion, language or continent.

The initial structure for the linear regression analysis consists in four different settings, analysing separately migration data by residence and by citizenship and then considering or not the Facebook SCI among the list of independent variables. The BMI indicator, representing the dependent variable, is then predicted for all the four settings following the backward elimination approach, which consists in the exclusion, at each step, of the variable considered to be the least relevant. At the end of all the necessary iterations, the final result for each one setting is a model with a reduced list of variables (i.e., those considered to be the most significant).

The results are summarised in Figure 2, where the initial and the final models are reported for each of the four configurations, including the p-values for each variable as a measure of its relevance. Beside noticing a strong improvement in the R^2 measure for those settings that take into account the Facebook SCI, this feature itself proves to be always strongly and positively significant.

Further detail of the evidence obtained during this phase can be observed in Figure 3, where the result of the best OLS model for migration data by residence is reported, corresponding to the linear regression described in the last column of Figure 2. The plot shows a comparison between the true and the estimated values of the BMI indicator related to 2019, also including information about SCI. Facebook strength of connectivity between two countries is strongly and positively related to the amount of migration flows they share. Moreover, the higher the connectivity the more accurate the migration prediction, as suggested by the match between color scale and linear growth.

Future work

The ultimate goal of our analysis is to integrate migration drivers with knowledge about past migration flows to build models able to nowcast and forecast migration. We will investigate and test different kinds of Machine Learning models in order to determine the best one in terms of performance outcomes and suitability with respect to our data and task. The different architectures that will be explored in this context are Random Forests, Support Vector Machines and Artificial Neural Networks (e.g., Multilayer Perceptron). The linear regression model we presented here will be employed to rank model features and feed into a filter feature selection method for the upcoming Machine Learning phase. In this way the non-relevant variables resulting from the fit of the OLS model will not be directly excluded, but p-values and coefficients will be exploited for feature ranking.

Figure 2. Results of OLS Backward Elimination Stepwise Linear Regression. Asterisks represent the relevance of each variable according to p-values, as illustrated above.

Y	By citizenship (148 couples, 14 countries)				By residence (1114 couples, 63 countries)			
	ESTAT BMI 2019 cit, without sci 2020		ESTAT BMI 2019 cit, with sci 2020		ESTAT BMI 2019 res, without sci 2020		ESTAT BMI 2019 res, with sci 2020	
Model n.	1	11	1	6	1	10	1	11
Feature	coef, P>|t|	coef, P>|t|	coef, P>|t|	coef, P>|t|	coef, P>|t|	coef, P>|t|	coef, P>|t|	coef, P>|t|
Intercept	-0.0005		0.0409 ***	0.0412 ***	0.0187 ***	0.0210 ***	0.1079 ***	0.1075 ***
sci_2020			0.0438 ***	0.0438 ***			0.1090 ***	0.1092 ***
geodesic_distance_km	-0.0161 **	-0.0114 ***	-0.0023	-0.0021	-0.0025		9.253e-05	
gdp_diff_2018	0.0074 **	0.0064 **	0.0032 ***	0.0033 ***	0.0040 ***	0.0039 ***	0.0018 ***	0.0016 ***
gdp_mean_2018	-0.0091 *	-0.0074 **	-0.0117 ***	-0.0116 ***	0.0058 ***	0.0055 ***	0.0005	
neighbours	0.0075 **	0.0081 ***	-0.0021 *	-0.0020 **	0.0138 ***	0.0140 ***	-0.0011	-0.0012 *
share_rel	0.0078 ***	0.0070 ***	0.0014	0.0013	0.0006		-0.0005 *	-0.0005 *
share_lang	-0.0024		-0.0013 *	-0.0014 **	0.0020 ***	0.0020 ***	0.0004	0.0004
PDI_diff	-0.0038	-0.0034	0.0020	0.0020	-0.0025 *	-0.0026 *	-0.0006	
IDV_diff	-0.0067 **	-0.0065 **	-0.0021 *	-0.0021 *	-0.0012		-0.0017 ***	-0.0017 ***
UAI_diff	0.0014		-0.0033 *	-0.0033 *	0.0003		0.0006	
MAS_diff	-0.0103 ***	-0.0088 ***	-0.0021 *	-0.0021 *	-0.0051 ***	-0.0050 ***	-0.0017 ***	-0.0018 ***
fb_users_diff	-0.0018		-0.0023 *	-0.0024 ***	0.0066	0.0068	-0.0007	
fb_users_perc_diff	0.0025		0.0043 ***	0.0044 ***	-0.0006		-8.071e-05	
fb_users_perc_mean	0.0028	0.0049	0.0025	0.0026 *	0.0054 ***	0.0055 ***	0.0044 ***	0.0047 ***
fb_users_mean	-0.0134 **	-0.0145 ***	-0.0005		-0.0114 *	-0.0112 *	-0.0010	-0.0016 **
area_diff	-0.0019		0.0002		-0.0029		0.0012	
area_mean	0.0036		0.0004		0.0034		-0.0011	
share_cont	0.0005				0.0047 ***	0.0063 ***	0.0010	0.0011 ***
R2 (centered)	0.574	0.560	0.949	0.949	0.363	0.361	0.880	0.880
AIC	-846.3	-855.7	-1158.	-1164.	-6321.	-6332.	-8179.	-8191.
BIC	-795.4	-825.7	-1104.	-1119.	-6231.	-6276.	-8084.	-8136.

Conclusion

All in all, our contributions lie in the need for new perspectives, methods, and analyses that can no longer prescind from taking into account a variety of new factors. The heterogeneous and multidimensional sets of data released with MIMI and exploited in the models with the aid of the BMI indicator offer a new overview of the characteristics of human migration, enabling a better understanding and a potential exploration of the relationship between migration and its drivers also through non-traditional sources of data.

Figure 3. BMI 2019 of EUROSTAT migration flows by residence: comparison between true values and linear regression predictions. This plot refers to the best fit obtained with the linear regression, i.e., the OLS model with $R^2 = 0.88$ corresponding to the last column in Figure 2. Each data point in the plot represents a country pair.

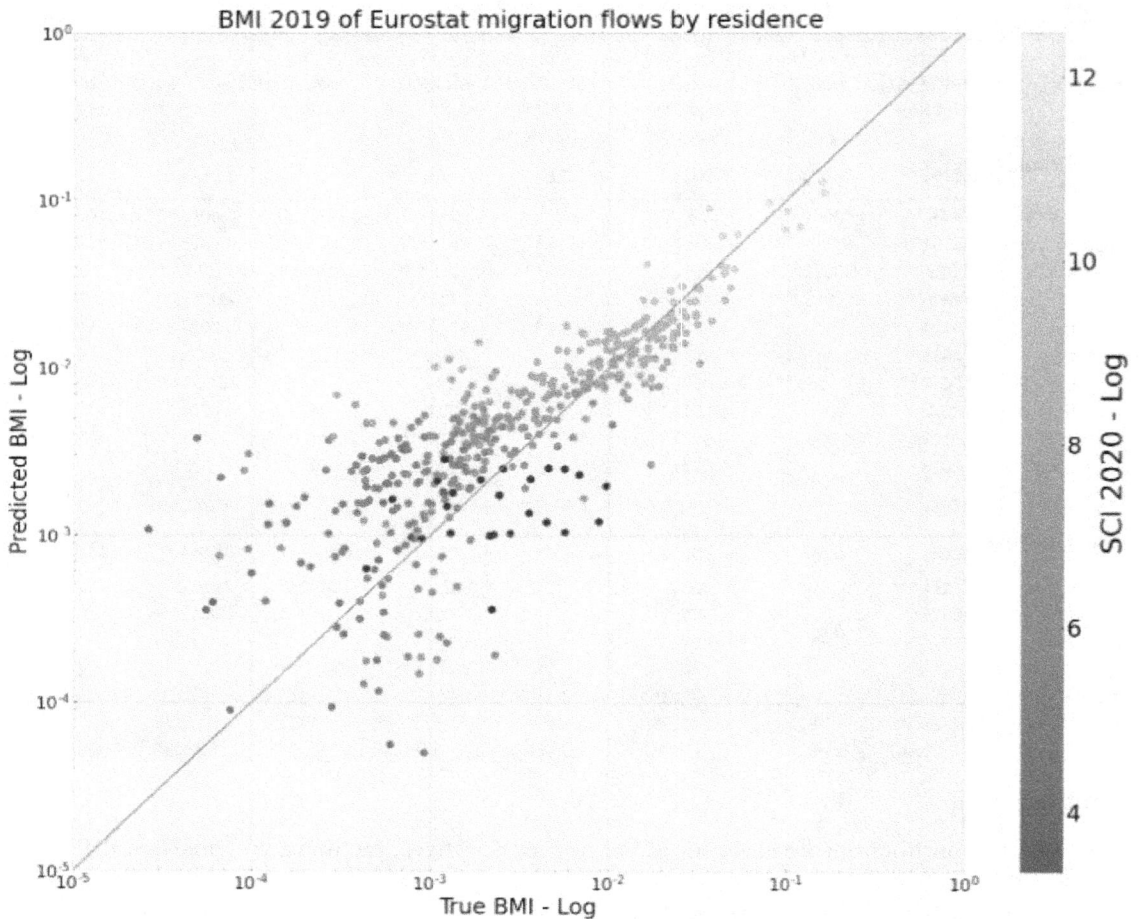

References

Bosco, C., Grubanov-Boskovic, S., Iacus, S., Minora, U., Sermi, F., & Spyratos, S. (2022). Data innovation in demography, migration and human mobility. DOI: 10.2760/958409 Fiorio, L., Abel, G., Cai, J., Zagheni, E., Weber, I., & Vinué, G. (2017). Using twitter data to estimate the relationship between short-term mobility and long-term migration. New York, NY, USA: Association for Computing Machinery.

Gendronneau, C., Yıldız, D., Hsiao, Y., Stepanek, M., Abel, G., Hoorens, S., Weber, I. (2019). Measuring labour mobility and migration using big data - exploring the potential of social-media data for measuring eu mobility flows and stocks of eu movers. Publications Office of the European Union.

Goglia, D. (2022, March). Multi-aspect Integrated Migration Indicators (MIMI) dataset. Zenodo. DOI: 10.5281/zenodo. 6493325

Goglia, D., Pollacci, L., & Sirbu, A. (2022). Dataset of multi-aspect integrated migration indicators. DOI: 10.48550/arXiv. 2204.14223

Kim, J., Sîrbu, A., Rossetti, G., Giannotti, F., & Rapoport, H. (2021). Home and destination attachment: study of cultural integration on twitter. arXiv. DOI:10.48550/ARXIV.2102.11398 Meta. (2021). Social connectedness index. https://bit.ly/SCIdataset. ([Online; accessed December 2021.])

Pollacci, L., Milli, L., Bircan, T., & Rossetti, G. (2022). Academic mobility from a big data perspective. DOI: 10.21203/rs.3.rs-1510153/v1

Salah, A. A. (2021). Chapter 8: Mobile data challenges for human mobility analysis and humanitarian response. In Research handbook on international migration and digital technology. Cheltenham, UK: Edward Elgar Publishing. DOI: 10.4337/9781839100611.00017

Spyratos, S., Vespe, M., Natale, F., Weber, I., Zagheni, E., & Rango, M. (2018). Migration data using social media: a european perspective. Publications Office of the European Union.

Sîrbu, A., Andrienko, G., Andrienko, N., Boldrini, C., Conti, M., Giannotti, F., Sharma, R. (2021). Human migration: the big data perspective. International Journal of Data Science and Analytics, 11(4), 341-360. DOI: 10.1007/s41060-020-00213-5

Zagheni, E., Garimella, V. R. K., Weber, I., & State, B. (2014). Inferring international and internal migration patterns from twitter data. New York, NY, USA: Association for Computing Machinery.

Zagheni, E., Polimis, K., Alexander, M., Weber, I., & Billari, F. C. (2018, 6). Combining social media data and traditional surveys to estimate and predict migration stocks. EAPS.

Zagheni, E., Weber, I., & Gummadi, K. (2017). Leveraging facebook's advertising platform to monitor stocks of migrants. Population and Development Review (4), 721–734.

MAPPING ENVIRONMENTAL RACISM: HYDROELECTRIC POWER AND THE ONGOING DISPLACEMENT OF MAROON-DESCENDED COMMUNITIES IN VALE DO RIBEIRA, BRAZIL

Diego de Jesus Santos[3]

Introduction

The twelve hydrographic regions located in Brazilian territory occupy an area of more than eight million square kilometers. They permeate metropolises and rural areas, forest areas and reserves, are the main source of income for riverside communities, support the livelihood of indigenous peoples, provide water for the agricultural industry or agricultural products, and bring electricity to the homes of millions of Brazilians through the production of hydraulic energy generated through water flows. The river, therefore, has outsize geographical impact, and I also think of the river as a methodology for a geohistory written in the course of its waters, recounting lives and livelihoods, and taking us through a Brazil which is shaped by the banks of its rivers and seas.

The Ribeira River, located in the Vale do Ribeira region, is my reference for writing part of the recent history of Brazil through the struggle of *quilombola*, or maroon-descended people, for the guarantee of land rights, as well as for the possibility of telling the history of Black movements in the territories of quilombo remnants (in a literal translation of the Portuguese *remanescentes de quilombos*). Measuring around 470 square kilometers, the Ribeira River bathes quilombos, riverside communities, indigenous lands and municipalities located between the states of São Paulo and Paraná. The region has 2 million hectares of Atlantic forest and an archaeological site with around 200 caves. The Ribeira Valley, considered a National Heritage Site and Natural Heritage of Humanity by UNESCO, is formed by the presence of 33 quilombola communities, ten Guarani villages and a Caiçara (riverine fishing) community. A total of 31 municipalities make up the territory where around 400,000 people currently live.

My study analyzes the context of the construction project of the Tijuco Alto Hydroelectric Power Plant in the region of Vale do Ribeira. My analysis turns to the migratory movement of the quilombola population in the region, threatened by the construction of dams along the Ribeira River basin and by the imminent installation of the hydroelectric plant. I analyze materials from the Quilombos of Vale do Ribeira Collection, available at the Lozano Long Institute of Latin American Studies/Benson Latin American Studies and Collections (The University of Texas at Austin), to build a chronology of the struggle against the construction of the dam in the period between 1989 and 2021. I examine the main challenges faced by the Movement of People Threatened by Dams - MOAB (Movimento dos Ameaçados por Barragens), created in 1989. My study aims to identify, through the elaboration of a map of environmental racism[4], the locations most affected by the Tijuco Alto Hydroelectric Power Plant project and by the current environmental legislation that criminalizes local means of production.

[3] PhD student, Department of Spanish and Portuguese, The University of Texas at Austin. diegojesus@utexas.edu. This research has been supported by the 2022 LLILAS Benson Digital Scholarship Fellowship, funded by the Mellon Post-custodial Collections Scholarly Engagement Grant.
[4] The map of environmental racism produced by this study in a partnership with EAACONE, as well as an interview with Tania Heloisa de Moraes from Vale do Ribeira and a professional involved in the maroon-descended movement for more than 10 years, can be found in a StoryMap JS link listed on the reference list of this paper.

For this, I discuss the concept of extractivism and question the Brazilian government's actions against the sustainable use of natural resources in the region by the residents.

Displaced Citizenship: A Mobile Archive of Black Struggle

MOAB was created to fight against the government's intention to build the Tijuco Alto Hydroelectric Power Plant in the territory where quilombola communities, indigenous and Caiçara lands are located. In 2016, the movement won in court, almost 30 years after its creation, bringing about the termination of the hydroelectric construction project. By examining their struggle, we can map the state-private sector project of environmental racism onto the region and the sites of its natural resources. The lengthy wait for an answer from the justice system also revealed the ongoing threat to the permanence[5] of residents of remaining quilombola communities and indigenous lands located in that territory. The plant's construction project involved the forced migration of part of the Black and indigenous populations either to slums and outskirts of large metropolises or small cities neighboring the forest areas where they were previously located. Despite several threats and persecution, the residents organized themselves into a movement that produced an archive of Black and indigenous struggle. Among these materials are letters to the government, the articulation of different demands by the population, protest organization, and the judicial action of the movement created by civil society against the plant project. Based on the concept of a "horizon of death" (Ferreira da Silva, 2009), I argue that the vulnerability of Black and indigenous bodies begins in the project of forced migration of these populations and their ancestors through the application of "slow violence" (Nixon, 2013). The deterritorialization project works for the maintenance of the racist structures that geographically and culturally compose anti-black and anti-indigenous neoliberal metropolises, which have always been devoid of what I call right to permanence. The nation-state project that produces the anti-black and anti-indigenous metropolis feeds on the displacement and extermination of these populations in the country's interior, depending on the act of making them, above all, "fugitives," homeless, without land, without rights, that is, devoid of humanity—a "social death" (Patterson, 2018) composed of the physical and social death of bodies devoid of citizenship. My study maps environmental racism and the struggle of the residents of Vale do Ribeira against the construction of the hydroelectric plant to expose the impacts of environmental racism in the region and to trace the migratory phenomenon of residents of rural areas and forest reserves to the periphery of different Brazilian cities.

Remaining communities of quilombos and indigenous territories have long been threatened by the Tijuco Alto Hydroelectric Power Plant project, whose installment was planned along the Ribeira River basin since 1989. Although, as previously mentioned, the Ministry of Mines and Energy ended the construction project of the power plant in 2016, as a result of the struggle of the MOAB and residents of the Vale do Ribeira region, residents continue to be threatened by new dam construction projects. The strategy now is to install Small Hydropower Plants (SHPs) in the Ribeira River basin, a legally viable measure due to a breach in environmental legislation.

In addition to documenting the MOAB's struggle, my study analyzes the map of environmental racism produced in partnership with the Team of Articulation and Advisory Services to the Rural Black Communities of Vale do Ribeira SP/PR - EAACONE, elaborated specifically for this study. From the elaboration and analysis of the map, my study highlights how the project to install the hydroelectric plant produced, in addition to other transformations in local daily life, the exodus of residents to territories adjoining the Ribeira Valley, or places further afield in the region. These residents were

---

[5] See Campos, 2005 and Leu (2020) on the extent to which Black struggle and resistance in Brazil are based on the fight for permanence in space. [Andrelino Campos, Do Quilombo à Favela, p. 31 & Leu, Defiant Geographies, especially the Epilogue on "the politics of staying put."

forced to migrate to large cities because of local persecution against resistance to a neoliberal developmental logic, as well as the scarcity of resources due to threats by inspection agencies which criminalize traditional extractive practices that guarantee the livelihood of a large part of the population. Forced displacement, as a neocolonial strategy of domination and exploitation, produces a supposedly unoccupied land to be exploited by the 21st century "settler," one who promises economic progress at the cost of dispossession, criminalization and exploitation of traditional communities.

The River as a Methodology for the Elaboration of a Black Memory Narrative

The application of violence is also channeled through forced displacements, that is, a displacement that is not only subjective, but also corporeal: The production of a fugitive body. Environmental racism, through the application of public policies developed by the state, ends up forcing remnants of quilombolas to migrate to urban areas and experience the lethal violence of the "anti-black city" (Alves, 2014). This text argues for the importance of documenting the fugitive movement and struggle of the displaced and those who experience "displacement without moving," Rob Nixon's term for a community that becomes "refugees in place" when it becomes too difficult to live on the land (2011, p. 19).

The method adopted by my study denounces, through the mapping of the environmental racism project, the threat to biodiversity and the permanence of residents in traditional communities located in the region of Vale do Ribeira. On the map, the possible consequences of the construction of the power plants predicted by the MOAB are listed and geographically identified, such as deforestation, deviations in the course of the Ribeira River, flooding of traditional communities and part of the forest reserves where they are located, as well as the socioeconomic impacts.

The map of environmental racism was drawn from the thematic maps produced for the construction of the SHPs as well as those used in the construction project of the Tijuco Alto power plant. This information was collected in documents of environmental licensing available on the Integrated Environmental Management System (SIGA), administered by the Brazilian Institute of Environment and Renewable Natural Resources (IBAMA), a federal agency under the Ministry of Environment. My study appropriates the data produced by a federal agency and crosses this information with the archive of struggle elaborated by the quilombola communities in Vale do Ribeira.

Although the Brazilian government has not yet demarcated and titled part of the quilombola lands threatened by the construction of power plants, the map of environmental racism shows the location of these spaces. The method developed in this study can be applied to rivers located in different quilombola lands located in Brazilian territory threatened by projects based on the practice of environmental racism, with the intention of telling the story of these black populations from their relationships with the river, be they socioeconomic, cultural, and spiritual.

The black riverine poesis in this relationship with the river aligns itself with the relationship of the black body with the ocean, expanding the look at black anthologies, by understanding the river as an element for the construction of a narrative of black struggle and black narrative.

Conclusion

The map of environmental racism not only identifies the social and economic issues posed by the construction of the power plants, but also presents a territory that expresses deep transformations in its cultural context, which indicate the impossibility of telling the story or following the story. For this reason, the chronology of the MOAB's struggle is essential to understand which aspects of this history need to be considered in order to think about the dimension of a project that, in addition to affecting natural resources, also produces an impossibility of archiving black and indigenous histories.

Displacement is itself what I classify in this study as violence on the move: It depends on forced movement so that the body is immersed in more violence, whether in rural areas or in large cities, in precarious life situations imposed by the need to migrate. In addition to the physical displacement, there are nuances of this experience that produce the subjective and, consequently, cultural displacement of the experience of the body that moves—not just in a physical dimension, that is, passive, the one that imposes on the body the condition of a living death, but also in the production of an inevitable social death, implied by the body that moves and that produces a movement of change through its decision to fight for locomotion, which will guarantee, or not, its survival.

References

Alves, J. (2018). *The Anti-Black City: Police Terror and Black Urban Life in Brazil*. Minneapolis, MN: University of Minnesota Press.

Campos, A. (2005). *Do Quilombo à Favela*. Rio de Janeiro, RJ: Bertrand Brasil.

de Jesus Santos, D., & EAACONE. (2022). Map of Environmental Racism – Vale do Ribeira, Brazil [Map]. StoryMap JS. https://uploads.knightlab.com/storymapjs/d2f7bf8d24b5c228e33a6d8307cc41b5/vale-do-ribeira/index.html.

Fanon, F. (1963). *The Wretched of the Earth*. New York, NY: Grove Press.

Ferreira da Silva, D. (2009). "No-Bodies": Law, Raciality and Violence. *Griffith Law Review*, *18*(2), 212–236. https://doi.org/10.1080/10383441.2009.10854638

Jeronymo, A. C. J., Bermann, C., & Guerra, S. M. (2012). "Displacements, Itineraries and Destinations of Populations Affected by Dams": HP Tijuco Alto, SP - PR. *Desenvolvimento e Meio Ambiente*, *25*, 133-152. http://dx.doi.org/10.5380/dma.v25i0.25273

Leu, L. (2020). *Defiant Geographies*. Pittsburgh, PA: University of Pittsburgh Press.

LLILAS Benson Latin American Studies and Collections (The University of Texas at Austin/University of Texas Libraries). (2022). *Quilombos of Vale do Ribeira Collection (Primary Sources)*. Retrieved from https://ladi.lib.utexas.edu/en/eaacone01

Nixon, R. (2011). *Slow Violence and the Environmentalism of the Poor*. Cambridge, MA: Harvard University Press.

Patterson, O. (2018). *Slavery and Social Death: A Comparative Study*. Cambridge, MA: Harvard University Press.

Pinto, M. A. M. (2014). *MOAB: A Saga de Um Povo*. Eldorado, SP: MOAB/EAACONE.

Roberts, N. (2015). Freedom as Marronages.

DE-MIGRANTICIZING MIGRANCY: APPROACHING MIGRATION AND (IN)MOBILITY ANALYSIS THROUGH RHIZOMATIC THINKING, FEMINIST EPISTEMES AND THE EMBODIED EXPERIENCE OF MIGRATION

Renato de Almeida Arão Galhardi[1]

Introduction

Despite the widely accepted argument to abandon methodological nationalism in international migration analysis (Wimmer and Schiller, 2003), much of the analysis that primes migration policies around the world still speak through the Nation-State (Bommes and Thränhardt, 2012; Dahinden, 2016). How, then, can migration research attend and attest to the critique of methodological nationalism? One way to do so is to de-migranticize migration analysis. By taking feminist epistemologies and methodologies seriously in migration analysis, and thinking "rhizomatically", it becomes possible to de-centre epistemic normative reproductions of migration descriptions, and create better narratives of migration phenomena, that embody migration over national methodological constraints and frameworks.

By maintaining discourses that do not "descend" from the lenses of the Nation-State and its legal body, narratives *hover* above the "migrant body" with the effect of naturalizing approaches to analyses, that reproduces hegemonic world-system views of migration and mobility. This "tyranny of the national" approach frequently dismisses issues of agency in favour of structure, and is prone to what Alex Sager (2014) has called "descriptive and explanatory inadequacy" while also being a testament to the perseverance of methodological frameworks that have become naturalized in migration research. Discourses that keep a "safe distance" from the migrant body are non-reflexive stances that are often moving within the boundaries of what Michael Shapiro (1997) calls "moral geography", that is, "a set of silent ethical assertions that preorganized explicit ethicopolitical discourses" (p. 16).

Significant efforts at the end of last century were made to decentre state-centrism from international migration discourse, notably by working through analytical frameworks such as transnationalism and its theoretical tributaries (Levitt and Jaworsky, 2007). Nevertheless, as Pessar and Mahler (2003) suggest, it still falters in addressing substantive aspects of the intersectional constitution of the "migrant body" such as gender and ethnicity, among others aspects highlighted by feminist epistemologies and methodologies, that structure the phenomenological positioning of "being-in-the-world" (Schües, 2018). In a similar tone to the call to "open up social sciences" in late 20th century (Wallerstein *et al.*, 1996), a growing number of migration research scholars have increasingly called for a greater appraisal of reflexivity in migration research in order to "tilt the frame"[2] of prevailing discourse (Shinozaki,

---

[1] Ph.D. candidate in Social and Political Sciences at the Universidad Iberoamericana, Mexico City. renato.almeida@correo.uia.mx. Fellow of Mexico's National Council for Science and Technology (CONACYT).
[2] See Steinberg, 1998.

2021)[3].

Feminist phenomenology and thinking through the body

It is precisely the intersectional complexity of experiences of migration -*its phenomenological properties*- that has eluded its encapsulation in a semantic articulation that can, effectively, denote key aspects of experiencing the experience of migration (Coole and Frost, 2010). One way to engage with the experience of migration, and bring the analytical value of experience to migration and mobility studies, is to take key from feminist phenomenology and think "through the body". Phenomenological consideration from feminist critical thought is crucial to rethink, de-naturalize and de-migranticize migration research. Linda Fisher (2000a) echoes this stance by stating that "the intertwining of feminist and phenomenological ideas has rich possibilities for a wide variety of fields and discussions, offering the potential of a suggestive, salutary, and radical analysis for future inquiry" (p. 15).

Within a discussion on the politics of technological subjugation in gender, Haraway (1997) alludes to the attachment necessary to situate the body as an embodied body, and does so -in part- through a creative usage of the theoretical consideration of prosthesis. By seeking a political and epistemological positioning of the body as "always a complex, contradictory, structuring, and structured body" as opposed to "the view from above, from nowhere, from simplicity" she is calling for an increase in the complexity of the subject, and ultimately placing the notions of gendered bodies as an intersecting social fact (p. 291). Ultimately, Haraway is expressing the *ontopological* property of migrancy. An ontopology, argues Jacques Derrida (1994) is the

> axiomatics linking indissociably the ontological value of present-being [*on*] to its *situation*, to the stable and presentable determination of a locality, the *topos* of territory, native soil, city, body in general) (p. 103).

Then, the experience of migration is a *situated experience within the experience of migration* mediated, precisely, due to its social construction and characteristics, determined by its *ontopological character*. To think of migrancy as ontopologically constituted is to make the body visible (Merleau-Ponty, 2002).

Embodying migrancy

Migrancy has frequently been reduced to convey something akin to the movement of migration as a lexical verb, commonly fashioned as a naturalized aspect of addressing facets of migration and mobility. This naturalized notion of migrancy, however, fails to attend to the necessary complexity embedded - and embodied- in migrancy. Embodying migrancy and migrating analysis has important implications for migration research. Taking Dahinden's "plea" to de-migranticize migration analysis seriously, a turn to Iain Chambers' (1994) seminal work on migrancy can recentre migrancy "through the body" and decentre migration analysis from normative "top down" approaches. Attending to the necessary complexity of migration phenomena -one that speaks to the holistic coupling of "seeing" migration with the migrant bodies that populate the phenomena- not only has the effect of humanizing migration discourse, but is also a fundamental turn to portray migration compassionately. Macro theories and structural approaches to migration analysis can benefit from feminist epistemologies that push for a greater consideration of the body -its place, participation, impact, shape, form, etc.- in migration analysis. To address gendered migration, for example, is but one may analyse can better represent migration phenomena. The push for embodiment is to shift the focus of migration discourse, narrative and forms of "seeing" migration phenomena from voices from "above" to voices from "below", creating a "third view". A "third view", in this case, can be achieved through a heterophenomenological

---

[3] See Schües, 2018.

approach.

Assuming a heterophenomenological stance allows us to treat narratives as stories that make sense of the world, and to take subjects "seriously" (Dennet, 1991). Considering the ontopological position and heterophenomenological condition of narrating migration and (in)mobility phenomena is a recognition of dialectics of identity as common denominators in the process of "seeing and describing" (social) reality (Kohl and McCutcheon, 2014). The explicit recognition of differentiation -the differences in "structural other-ness" that shape identity politics (Braidotti, 2006) - allows migration discourse to highlight the heterogeneity of the plights of migrants and pry away from normalization and naturalisation discourses that "hover" above the migration field. Given this, I propose understanding migrancy, with and through its reflexive and positionality properties, as the *"the (unfinished) social product of the social process of the experience of migration, heterophenomenologically expressed and ontopologically situated".* De-migranticizing migrancy brings the patriarchal heteronormative domestication of alternative forms and systems of being, into the dominated relation it occurs in.

Rhizomatic thinking and embodied migrancy: Thinking in multiplicity

As Deleuze and Guattari (1987) point out, the arborescent structure of the genealogy of normative epistemic expressions stems from a centre that denies the multiplicity of beginnings. To re-rethink from different centres is one of the methodological premises of critical feminist thought, and the precursor to engage reflexively on and through positionality. It is a demand to escape the mimesis of thought and engage in a "radical" -as the return to the root- mode of thinking.

Seeking to reverse the arborescent epistemological model - *to turn the world upside down* - Deleuze and Guattari propose an "inverse" methodological perspective, which seeks to divert the "upwards" naturalized gaze – from the trunk of tree, its foliage and canopy- "downwards", through the soil toward the radicle-system of the rhizome. Gilles Deleuze and Felix Guattari are, effectively, suggesting a rupture to the order of subjugation of implicit hierarchies of thinking. This gives rise to *rhizomatic thinking*. Rhizomes, argue the authors, are non-subjugated ways of engaging with ideas; it is, inherently, a path toward non-linear movement in engaging with thought, whereby the product of creation is not the sum of its properties but the *state of its multiplicity*.

Rhizomatic thinking is the essence of innovation of the forms of approaching objects of analysis of importance to the state of migration and mobilities research. As case in point, Rosi Braidotti (1997) has called rhizomatic thinking a *nomadic style*, to reference the itinerant movement between the positionality of the enunciation and interpretation, as forms of interpreting and observing. In her own words, Rosi Braidotti (1997) states that a nomadic style, as in the case with rhizomatic thinking, "implies the simultaneous dislocation not only of my place of enunciation as a feminist intellectual but also accordingly of the position of my readers" (p. 60). To embody migration analysis, then, is a pursuit for a more just description that "sees" the migrant.

References

Bommes, M., and Thränhardt, D. (2012). National paradigms of migration research. In *Immigration and social systems: Collected essays of Michael Bommes*. Amsterdam University Press. pp. 201-232. https://doi.org/10.1515/9789048517299-012

Braidotti, R. (1997). Mothers, Monsters, and Machines. In *Writing on the body: female embodiment and feminist theory*. New York: Columbia University Press.

Braidotti, R. (2006). *Transpositions: on nomadic ethics*. Cambridge: Polity Press.

Chambers, I. (1994). *Migrancy, culture, identity*. Routledge.

Coole, D., and Frost, S. (2010). Introducing the new materialisms. *New materialisms: Ontology, agency, and politics*, 1-43. https://doi.org/10.1215/9780822392996-001

Dahinden, J., (2016). A plea for the 'de-migranticization'of research on migration and integration. *Ethnic and Racial Studies,*

39(13), pp. 2207-2225. https://doi.org/10.1080/01419870.2015.1124129

Deleuze, G., and Guattari, F. (1987). *A thousand plateaus: Capitalism and Schizophrenia*. University of Minnesota Press.

Dennett, D.C. (1991). *Consciousness explained*. London: Penguin.

Derrida, J. (1994). Specters of Marx: The State of the Debt, The Work of Mourning, and The New International. New York: Routledge.

Fisher, K. T. (2014). Positionality, subjectivity, and race in transnational and transcultural geographical research. *Gender, Place & Culture, 22*(4), pp. 456–473. https://doi.org/10.1080/0966369X.2013.879097

Fisher, L. (2000a). Feminist Phenomenology. In *Feminist Phenomenology*, pp. 1–15. https://doi.org/10.1007/978-94-015-9488-2_1

Gatens, M. (1997). Corporeal Representation in /a n d the Body Politic. In *Writing on the body: female embodiment and feminist theory*. New York: Columbia University Press.

Guillaumin, C. (1995). *Racism, sexism, power and ideology*. Routledge.

Haraway, D. (1988). Situated Knowledges: The Science Question in Feminism and the Privilege of Partial Perspective. *Feminist Studies, 14*(3), pp. 575–599. https://doi.org/10.2307/3178066

Kohl, E. and McCutcheon, P. (2014). Kitchen table reflexivity: negotiating positionality through everyday talk. *Gender, Place & Culture, 22*(6), pp. 747–763. https://doi.org/10.1080/0966369X.2014.958063

Levitt, P. and Jaworsky, B. N. (2007). Transnational Migration Studies: Past Developments and Future Trends. *Annual Review of Sociology, 33*, 129–56. https://doi.org/10.1146/annurev.soc.33.040406.131816

Merleau-Ponty, M. (2002). *Phenomenology of Perception*. London: Routledge. https://doi.org/10.4324/9780203994610

Nail, T. (2015). *The figure of the migrant*. Stanford University Press. https://doi.org/10.1515/9780804796682

Pessar, P. R., and Mahler, S. J. (2003). Transnational Migration: Bringing Gender In. International *Migration Review, 37*(3), 812–846. https://doi.org/10.1111/j.1747-7379.2003.tb00159.x

Sager, A. (2014). Methodological Nationalism, Migration and Political Theory. *Political Studies*. SAGE Publications. https://doi.org/10.1111/1467-9248.12167.

Schües, C., (2018). Phenomenology and politics: Injustice and prejudices. *Rethinking feminist phenomenology: Theoretical and applied perspectives*, New York: Rowman & Littlefield International, pp. 103-120.

Seamon, D. (2018). Merleau-Ponty, Lived Body, and Place: Toward a Phenomenology of Human Situatedness. *Contributions To Phenomenology*, pp. 41–66. https://doi.org/10.1007/978-3-319-92937-8_4

Shapiro, M.J. (1997). *Violent cartographies: mapping cultures of war*. Minneapolis: University of Minnesota Press.

Shinozaki, K. (2021). Reflexivity and Its Enactment Potential in Gender and Migration Research. In *The Palgrave Handbook of Gender and Migration*. Springer International Publishing. https://doi.org/10.1007/978-3-030-63347-9_6

Steinberg, M. W. (1998). Tilting the frame: Considerations on collective action framing from a discursive turn. *Theory and society, 27*(6), pp. 845-872. https://doi.org/10.1023/A:1006975321345

Wimmer, A. and Schiller, N.G. (2003). Methodological nationalism, the social sciences, and the study of migration: An essay in historical epistemology. *International migration review, 37*(3), pp. 576-610. https://doi.org/10.1111/j.1747-7379.2003.tb00151.x

Wallerstein, I. (1989). 1968, Revolution in the world-system. *Theory and Society, 18*(4), 431–449. https://doi:10.1007/bf00136434

Wallerstein, I., Juma, C., Keller, E. F., Kocka, J., Lecourt, D., Mudkimbe, V. Y., Miushakoji, K., Prigogine, I., Taylor, P. J. and Trouillot, M.-R. (1996). *Open the social sciences: Report of the Gulbenkian Commission on the restructuring of the social sciences*. Stanford, CA: Stanford University Press. https://doi.org/10.1515/9781503616219

"WHY IS IT SO DIFFICULT TO CAPTURE A HYPER-MOBILE WORKFORCE? REFLECTIONS FROM FIELD RESEARCH ABOUT ATYPICAL MIGRATION IN POLAND"

Kamil Matuszczyk[1,2]

Introduction

While the size of migrant population in a particular country is portrayed as a 'hard-to-survey population', there are sectors where the very nature of the work and circumstances make it impossible to measure it (Massey 2014; Abrantes 2015), such as the household sector and agriculture. Temporariness, the need for flexibility, informality and labor intensiveness are features of this sector. Operating in the shadow economy makes it virtually impossible to estimate the number of foreign workers in these two sectors. This challenge is caused by the workers disappearing from the official registers and difficulties in empirical research. Certain daily practices make it impossible to measure how many workers work for a given employer at a time. However, explaining this methodological difficulty only with undeclared work in the informal economy is too general and impoverishes the understanding of hypermobility of workers in low-skilled labour (i.e. jobs characterised by low prestige, low salaries, ease of obtaining, lack of formal requirements for candidates' qualifications).

This paper aims to explain the difficulties in capturing a hypermobile workforce. By identifying the strategies undertaken by employers and mobile workers, I demonstrate how bottom-up activities condition the way labor mobility is identified in the low-skilled labour, using the example of posted workers from Poland in temporary domestic employment in Germany as well as of Ukrainian workers employed in agriculture in Poland.

Atypical labor migration within the EU

The free movement of workers is one of the pillars of the European Union, entitling citizens of the Member States to take up employment in other countries. Although this form of migration remains dominant, other forms of temporary labor mobility have been growing dynamically in the last two decades. Wagner and Hassel (2017) proposed an apt classification of these forms. Typical labor migration denotes a cross-border move for longer-term employment (i.e. more than 3 months), mainly based on the free movement of workers. Atypical labor migration is temporary and has specific restrictions. This form includes seasonal work, posting of workers (i.e. a situation where a worker in one EU or EEA country is temporarily deployed to perform services in another Member State) and self-employment. Importantly, workers keep the focus of their lives at home and work in the receiving country temporarily, without actually moving there (Arnholtz, Lillie 2020).

Atypical labor mobility is rising thanks to the possibility of earning relatively higher wages in one

---

[1] The article presents outcomes from research project "Care services provided to the elderly by foreigners in Poland and quality of home care - perspective of public policies" number 2017/27/N/HS5/00745, funded by National Science Centre, Poland (Preludium).
[2] Centre of Migration Research, University of Warsaw. kamil_t_matuszczyk@uw.edu.pl

country without permanent migration. It is mainly employers, taking advantage of the freedom of movement of services, who decide to delegate workers. Also, in agriculture, which strongly relies on foreign labor, unique solutions are used to enable employment, depending on the demand for work and employers' needs. Although employment regulations exist (Posting of Workers Directive 96/71 or Seasonal Workers Directive 2014/36), such practices create room for their numerous abuses. The practices used by employers, partly also by workers, create challenges in terms of accurately estimating the scale of seasonal migration in EU Member States or the volume of worker postings.

Scale of atypical labor migration to and from Poland

It is estimated that after Poland's accession to the EU in 2004, about 2.5 million people emigrated from Poland. However, this number does not include numerous circular departures (the so-called liquid migration), especially to Germany. Experts estimate at least 300,000 Polish workers find employment every year in private households in Germany. About 80% start work without the relevant formalities (e.g. registering residence or signing a contract with the employer) (Nowicka et al. 2021). A significant proportion of these are posted workers, mainly to Germany – mainly in construction, manufacturing, or personal services sectors (Arnholtz, Lillie 2020).

With the Russian aggression in Ukraine initiated in 2014, hundreds of thousands of immigrants come to Poland every year. From a typical emigration country, Poland became a New Immigration Destination country within a few years. Immigration to Poland is mainly temporary, seasonal in nature. Importantly, in 2018 Poland became the leader among OECD countries in attracting temporary workers, ahead of the US, Germany, France, and Canada (Fiałkowska, Matuszczyk 2021). With the above in mind, Poland has in recent years become the leading country receiving and sending workers under the so-called atypical labor migration.

Methods and data source

To answer the research question, this paper refers the results of three empirical research projects on atypical labor migration to and from Poland. The three projects are summarized in Table 1.

Table 1. Summary of research projects used in this paper

	Care services for the elderly provided by foreigners and the quality of home care - a public policy perspective	Poland's policy on international migration to the elderly care sector 2007-2018	Global Labor in Rural Societies (GLARUS):
Aim	capturing the logic of the care industry in Poland and the extent to which care migration from and to Poland is politicized	to identify to what extent care migration in Poland has become a crucial public issue	addresses the important but poorly explored question of how contemporary global flows of low-skilled and manual labor transform the social fabric of non-urban regions in Western society
Sample	Care agencies, policy makers, Polish migrant domestic workers	Policy makers, care agencies, care experts	Farmers, migrant farm workers
Methods	55 IDIs	10 IDIs	23 IDIs, approx. 80 days participant observations
Time	2018-2021	2019-2020	2019-2021
Funded by	Polish National Science Centre, Preludium scheme (2017/27/N/HS5/00745)	Polish National Science Centre, Etiuda scheme (2019/32/T/HS5/00131)	Norwegian Research Council and NTNU

With the presented characteristics of the implemented projects in mind, in the following I rely on original empirical material consisting of more than 80 in-depth interviews with employers (care agencies and farmers), employees (caregivers and farmworkers) and notes and interviews carried out during participant observation in 2019-2021 during joint fruit picking with Ukrainian employees in the Grójec district (50 km from Warsaw), referred to as the "fruit-growing basin of Europe".

Analysis: employers' and workers' strategies

The collected material revealed that despite specific regulations on atypical migration in Europe, employers in the home care or agriculture sector often use (or condone) informal or semi-formal strategies. This type of approach is mainly due, as repeatedly pointed out, to the increasing deficit of good workers willing to take up employment in low-prestige jobs. A significant proportion of the interviewees are aware of various practices and actions which consequently lead to the actual hiring scale being impossible to capture. Below are the main strategies that emerged from the interviews and participant observation.

Domestic care:

- Posting of workers without proper documents. Work in domestic service, as demonstrated by the research, often requires the worker's immediate provision. When receiving an offer from a German family (or brokering agencies in Germany co-operating with the sending agencies in Poland), the actors do their best to recruit, screen and dispatch the worker in the shortest time possible. Employers admit that there are exceptional situations when they post their workers without the relevant documents. The lack of qualified workers means that employers often, in order not to lose a good employee, agree to skip bureaucracy and send an employee without an A1 form or a European Health Insurance Card. Although such employees receive these documents, they may be employed in a grey area for several weeks.

- Job-hopping strategy. Interviews conducted with employees with experience of working in Germany for at least 12 months revealed that a frequent strategy, despite legal work through a posting agency from Poland, is very short trips and work as a substitute. The employees themselves described this strategy as "jumper work", which is possible mainly thanks to good knowledge of the realities of the German labor market, but also geographical proximity and developed migration infrastructure between the two countries. Asked by friends, experienced workers decide to work in Germany without any contract, usually for 1-3 weeks. This demonstrates the strength of the migration relationship and the maneuvering between legal employment and extremely short illegal work. The so-called "jumpers" are aware of the potential dangers and voluntarily decide to fall into the grey area. Thus, persons going to Germany do not appear in any registers, although formally they may be employed legally by Polish employment agencies.

Agriculture:

- Employment on a tourist visa. Thanks to changes in the migration law, Ukrainians can stay in the territory of Poland (and other EU countries) under the visa-free regime for up to 90 days. Their stay should be touristic, but in practice many decide to take up temporary employment in agriculture, where it is difficult to control the legality of their stay. Also, employers, experiencing a deficit of workers in the last few years, still accept the risk of employing people without the required work permits. This strategy is used by migrants who decide to work only for a few weeks. My research has confirmed that the strawberry harvest in May and June is a period of increased presence of migrants from Ukraine, including those working on tourist visas. Many of these people, as they confirm in interviews, decided to take a holiday in Ukraine and come to Poland undeclared. This was a strategy to maximize earnings, although legalizing residence is not costly. Moreover, participant observation at a farm in 2019 established that minors under the age of 15 were also working at the blueberry harvest. These children were staying on a tourist visa with their parents, who obtained permission from their employer to come with their children. They are not recorded in any register in receiving country.

- Working during mandatory quarantine. The COVID-19 pandemic revealed the creativity of workers and employers in circumventing restrictions and recommendations for work organization. It is noteworthy that by living on the farm, right next to the employer's house, workers were able to undertake paid work during the mandatory quarantine. Surveys conducted in 2020 and 2021, respectively, confirmed that this opportunity was seized by workers who had permission to work in other sectors than agriculture. For example, on the four orchard farms surveyed, there were Ukrainians going to work on construction sites. However, in order not to lose time during the mandatory quarantine (working on the construction site during quarantine was not possible), they decided to stay for a short time and work in agriculture. By working with informal intermediaries (drivers), such workers ended up in agriculture, without any documents. This is another example of functioning in the black economy for a short period, without the required formalities.

Summary

1. Poland has become a leader in atypical labor migration. Posting of workers and seasonal migration, although not a new form of economic mobility, are gaining interest among employers looking for a workforce for a limited period (mainly a few weeks or months).

2. Foreign employees in home care and agriculture fall out of official records because they (aided by employers) are using quasi-illegal strategies to circumvent the existing migration laws. For example, at the peak of the fruit harvest, it is possible to rely on additional workers who work on tourist visas.

3. Using the strategies described above is closely related to the specifics of the work and the terms and conditions of employment in domestic care and fruit picking. The dynamically changing demand for workers determines the implementation of measures that lead to an increase in the informal economy. Thus, it is virtually impossible to measure the number of workers at any given time. Being able to capture the scale of employment of workers in particular sectors means benefits for both the migrants themselves (e.g. including the ability to monitor their working conditions), but also for the effective management of labour migration.

References

Abrantes, M. (2014). What about the numbers? A quantitative contribution to the study of domestic services in Europe. *International Labour Review*, 153(2), 223–243. https://doi.org/10.1111/j.1564-913X.2014.00202.x

Arnholtz, J., & Lillie, N. (2020). European Integration and Reconfiguration of National Industrial Relations: Posted Worker as a Driver of Institutional Change, in: Arnholtz, J., & Lillie, N. (eds.), *Posted Work in the European Union. The Political Economy of Free Movement*, New York, London: Routledge, pp. 1–30.

Fiałkowska, K., & Matuszczyk, K. (2021). Safe and fruitful? Structural vulnerabilities in the experience of seasonal migrant workers in agriculture in Germany and Poland. *Safety Science*, 139, https://doi.org/10.1016/j.ssci.2021.105275.

Massey, D. S. (2014). Challenges to surveying immigrants, in: Tourangeau, R., Edwards, B., Johnson, T. P., Wolter, K. M., & Bates, N. (eds.), *Hard-to-Survey Populations,* Cambridge: Cambridge University Press, pp. 270–292.

Nowicka, M., Bartig, S., Schwass, T., & Matuszczyk, K. (2021). COVID-19 Pandemic and Resilience of the Transnational Home-Based Elder Care System between Poland and Germany. *Journal of Aging and Social Policy*, 33(4-5), 474-492. https://doi.org/10.1080/08959420.2021.1927615

Wagner, B., & Hassel, A. (2017). Move to Work, Move to Stay? Mapping Atypical Labour Migration into Germany, in: Dølvik,

J. E., & Eldring, L. (eds.), *Labour Mobility in the Enlarged Single European Market*, Bingley: Emerald Publishing, pp. 125–158.

ADDRESSING INEQUALITIES: THE COLLECTION OF RACE STATISTICS. A COMPARISON BETWEEN THE EUROPEAN AND THE BRITISH APPROACH TO POPULATION REGISTERS

Iris Egea Quijada

Introduction

Population registers collect relevant information about the migrant stock. Despite their formal formats, they are context-dependent and tied to the historical arrangements and social forces of each country (Simon, 2012). At the European level, there is no single approach to data collection. Recently, due to rising racism and inequalities, the collection of race statistics in population registers has triggered debate. In fact, in the field of migration studies, race is a highly contentious concept because its interpretation depends on specific contexts (Jacobs, 2018).

While in Britain (the United Kingdom), race is openly tackled, its use in continental Europe is mostly omitted. These opposing perspectives are also reflected in the population statistics. Britain has been collecting race information since the 1960s (Farkas, 2017). Contrarily, most of continental Europe does not use any mechanism that accounts for racial difference in their demographic statistics and, instead, migrant status acts as a proxy to race in population registers. Despite these opposing traditions, the reality shows that migrants – of colour generally – are racialised because their presence is perceived to be in opposition with the Western identity – linked to "whiteness" (De Genova, 2018). Hence, migrants' experience in Europe entails racism, discrimination and inequality. With the outbreak of COVID-19, the experience of vulnerability has been exacerbated by prominent health inequalities among people of colour (Waldersee, 2020). This has brought many actors to argue in favour of the collection of race statistics to monitor inequalities (Waldersee, 2020).

Regarding the topic's relevance, the aim of this paper is to discuss the role or absence of race in population registers by comparing the British and the European models in order to normatively address the inequalities and disadvantages that the migrant stock faces in Europe. Firstly, an introduction to the historical European racial background will be addressed. Secondly, the benefits and limitations of not accounting for race on racialised migrants' wellbeing will be reflected upon. Thirdly, the British approach will be analysed historically and its effects will be examined. Following that, the ethical considerations and the difficult inquiry of race as a socially constructed category will be addressed. Finally, taking the European diverse racial reality into account, the text will conclude by proposing a timely approach to population statistics based on the British model.

The European race-blind model

In continental Europe, the collection of data on race has historically been linked to the exclusion, discrimination and elimination by mass murder of individuals who have been perceived as undesired minorities at the hands of the colonial and the Nazi regimes (Seltzer, 1998 et al.; Möschel et al., 2013). Thus, after the Second World War, continental Europe stopped using race as an analytical category driven by the fear that such practice might trigger differential treatment (Möschel, 2011). The so-called colour/race-blind approach reflects an effort to eliminate racism advanced by the belief that the elimination of numerical analysis of racial features will make racism eventually disappear (Möschel, et al., 2013). Additionally, such information is often regarded as an inaccurate technique to define population and social developments forasmuch as they contest the representation of the ideal homogeneous European societies (Möschel et al., 2013). Some countries – mainly the Nordic countries – use proxies, such as collecting data on diversity by noting parents' place of birth and Eurostat follows that practice too. This practice responds to the fact that European countries are still considered "post-migration countries" after experiencing labour migration followed by family reunification during the second half of the twentieth century (Simon, 2012). Nevertheless, the continental European heterogeneous paradigm, even accounting for proxies, brings about limitations.

The absence of racial statistics especially affects racialised migrants in the social, political and legal dimensions. Regarding the social dimension, the common proxy of noting "migrant background" characteristics does not safeguard second, third and fourth generations, whose parents are European native-born but who are discriminated against because of their skin colour (Oltermann & Henley, 2020). Such an approach is also limited for individuals of mixed backgrounds (Farkas, 2017). Furthermore, identifying a native born with a foreign heritage makes governments mistakenly focus on integration rather than discrimination (Simon 2012). Concerning the political dimension, racialised individuals have been proven to be silenced in the democratic processes (Möschell et al., 2013). Moreover, by not taking race into consideration, European legal systems overlook the historical patterns of racial discrimination (Möschel et al., 2013). Indeed, the possibilities of obtaining justice when claiming discrimination are scarce. Consequently, the few reported cases of discrimination attributed to race do not reflect the real number of discriminatory acts (Möschell, 2011). Overall, legal systems mistakenly understand racism as perpetuated by a small minority (Möschell, 2011).

The British race-sensitive model

At the other side of the spectrum lies the British model, which has applied race into its population surveys since the 1960s (Farkas, 2017). The historical background to the British approach to race statistics is also worth to analyse. Despite sharing the colonial past with Europe, Britain holds a different approach to race. Britain soon started to receive migration from its former colonies from Ireland and its colonies in Africa, South Asia and the Caribbean in the post-war period (Geddes, 2004). After the 1948 British Nationality Act, those from the former colonies were allowed to settle in Britain and they became ethnic minorities (Geddes, 2004). Moreover, between 1780 and 1830, Black people were already living in Britain (Myers, 1996). The census forms include the following categories: "White, Mixed/Multiple ethnic groups, Asian/Asian British, Black/African /Caribbean/Black British, Other ethnic group" (Oltermann & Henley, 2020). These racial minorities have been officially protected from discrimination since 2010, when the Equality Act was approved to promote equal treatment in society (Laux, 2021). Race is one of the nine characteristics that is protected and "it includes (a) colour; (b) nationality; (c) ethnic or national origins" (Equality Act, 2010). In Britain, anti-racist struggles are associated with politics of citizenship (De Genova, 2018).

The British model has different effects in the social, political and, economic dimensions. Socially, the model is effective for measuring the level of integration of racial relations and safeguards racial specificities and, cultural, linguistic and religious identities (Makkonen, 2016). In the political domain, race statistics can provide the measurement of policy effectiveness and can recognise individuals of minority communities (Shendruk, 2021). Finally, the British model allows for officially and legally reporting race-related crimes (CRED, 2021).

Ethical concerns of race data collection

Nevertheless, collecting race statistics also has ethical implications. Most formal concerns are related to data protection, as it is often considered that racial origin is "sensitive data" (Kriszan, 2001 et al.; Möschel et al., 2013). That means that, as a socially constructed concept, race is a challenging indicator to be represented in demographic surveys (Simon, 2012). Its subjective, changing and open nature clashes with the delimited divisions of statistics. Thus, statistical categories do not allow individuals to be defined in between categories as they can only opt in or out of one (Simon, 2012). Because of its subjective nature, race is perceived differently according to one's point of view. In the British context, it has generally been self-reported (Race Disparity Unit, 2021). Nevertheless, race identification can result from self-categorisation, which reflects how one sees oneself, other-identification, how others perceive us, and perceived identification, how one believes others see us (Chopin, Farkas & Germaine, 2014). Its complexity makes it difficult to grasp in a normative way, for one can suffer discrimination according to a feature that has not been statistically registered or one might find it difficult to choose which racial profile describes them the best. Furthermore, some say that race is not enough for following-up with discriminatory situations across the social, political or legal dimensions because it might obscure inter-racial inequalities, e.g., Black Caribbean versus Black African (CSJ, 2020). Moreover, the "white working class" who has historically been socially disadvantaged has brought many to consider that the focus of equality statistics on racial minorities is not accurate, leaving some individuals unattended (CSJ, 2020).

Despite the limits, the British tradition of collecting race data has contributed to making the scrutiny of race relevant for population registers – among other sources of data, such as censuses. Every year the UK's Commission on Race and Ethnic Disparities issues a report covering the year's hate crimes and the latest shows that the majority of the hate crimes registered in 2018-19 were race-related, with 78,991 offences – accounting for 76% of the total claimed crimes (CRED, 2021). These worrying results show that race is still timely and undoubtedly relevant. It ultimately appeals to reconsider continental European population statistics.

However, the collection of race statistics does not automatically imply the use of it for a good/normative cause, i.e., the monitoring of inequality. It highly depends on the perspective taken and use made by the institution in charge (Simon, 2012). Nonetheless, collecting race statistics both shapes and reflects a reality where race relations are deemed important. Hence, race data collection can be organised under anti-discrimination statistics. In fact, while the British integration policy acknowledges the existence of racial groups, the race relations legislation prohibits both indirect and direct discrimination (Geddes, 2004). These registers establish a comparison between collectives allegedly exposed to inequalities and discrimination, and a benchmark which should not be prejudiced for on the field that is examined (Simon, 2012).

Conclusion

Overall, in order to create comparative European work in shaping effective equality policies, there must be a homogeneous European approach to data registration, whereby race is collected. The distinction should go beyond the dichotomy between nationals and non-nationals under the label of "migration background", as that would vary across Europe due to the important variations in nationality acquirement (Jacobs, 2018). This way, race will be approached normatively. In short, to fight the racism and racial discrimination that migrants are subject to, a race-blind or colour-blind approach is limited as it silences the reality – race still shapes one's identities and opportunities. On the contrary, one is "compelled to think racially" (Omi & Winant, 1994; De Genova, 2018).

References

Chopin, I., Farkas, L. & Germaine, C. (2014). *Equality Data Initiative ETHNIC ORIGIN AND DISABILITY DATA COLLECTION IN EUROPE: MEASURING INEQUALITY –*. *November*.

Commission on Race and Ethnic Disparities (CRED). (2021). *The Report*. *March*, 1–258.

CSJ. (2020). FACING THE FACTS: ETHNICITY AND DISADVANTAGE IN BRITAIN Disparities in education, work, and family. *The Centre for Social Justice, November*. www.centreforsocialjustice.org.uk@CSJthinktankwww.designbysoapbox.com

De Genova, N. (2018). The "migrant crisis" as racial crisis: do Black Lives Matter in Europe? *Ethnic and Racial Studies*, *41*(10), 1765–1782. https://doi.org/10.1080/01419870.2017.1361543

Farkas, L. (2017). Data collection in the field of ethnicity. In *Analysis and comparative review of equality data collection practices in the European Union*. https://www.google.com/%0Afile:///Users/kathrynschauer/Documents/Papers/Library.papers3/Files/1E/1EE4501F-72D7-4242-AA9D-F62B124260AB.pdf%0Apapers3://publication/uuid/CAED2C00-B7DD-4B7F-858F-7D64615F70A8

Geddes, A. (2004). Britain, France, and EU anti-discrimination policy: The emergence of an EU policy paradigm. *West European Politics*, *27*(2), 334–353. https://doi.org/10.1080/0140238042000214937

Laux, R. (2021, June 15). Asking people about their ethnicity. Retrieved from https://dataingovernment.blog.gov.uk/2021/06/15/asking-people-about-their-ethnicity/

Legislation.gov.uk. (2010). *Equality Act 2010*. [online] Retrieved from http://www.legislation.gov.uk/ukpga/2010/15/contents

Makkonen, T. (2016). *European handbook on equality data - 2016 revision*. http://ec.europa.eu/newsroom/just/item-detail.cfm?item_id=54849

Möschel, M. (2011). Race in mainland European legal analysis: Towards a European critical race theory. *Ethnic and Racial Studies*, *34*(10), 1648–1664. https://doi.org/10.1080/01419870.2011.566623

Möschel, M., Hermanin, C., & Grigolo, M. (2016). *Fighting discrimination in Europe: The case for a race-conscious approach*. London: Routledge.

Myers, N. & Myers, N. (1996). *Reconstructing the Black Past*. London: Routledge. https://doi.org/10.4324/9780203043929

Oltermann, P., & Henley, J. (2020, June 16). France and Germany urged to rethink reluctance to gather ethnicity data. Retrieved from https://www.theguardian.com/world/2020/jun/16/france-and-germany-urged-to-rethink-reluctance-to-gather-ethnicity-data?fbclid=IwAR1Y1KYuR5BrgwMQjDW0bfhFALyE93xGn75K1R9ej2V1lqN359iljQdYCUQ

Race Disparity Unit. (2021). Differences in the quality of ethnicity data reported by individuals and third parties. Retrieved from https://www.gov.uk/government/publications/differences-in-the-quality-of-ethnicity-data-reported-by-individuals-and-third-parties/differences-in-the-quality-of-ethnicity-data-reported-by-individuals-and-third-parties

Shendruk, A. (2021, July 8). Are you even trying to stop racism if you don't collect data on race? Retrieved from https://qz.com/2029525/the-20-countries-that-dont-collect-racial-and-ethnic-census-data/?fbclid=IwAR3tNqgoGrtIS8olEP40eWOdKa4vjvXhfN3bDSuzbuyuOYMzlB-x6oGN9ws

Simon, P. (2012). Collecting ethnic statistics in Europe: A review. *Ethnic and Racial Studies*, *35*(8), 1366–1391. https://doi.org/10.1080/01419870.2011.607507

Waldersee, V. (2020, November 19). COVID toll turns spotlight on Europe's taboo of data by race. Retrieved from https://www.reuters.com/article/uk-health-coronavirus-europe-data-insigh-idUKKBN27Z0K6?fbclid=IwAR18CJKbwj6cs6bM_R7AFae-r9fBDNmyXoOfs3P44CAzaqsp576pKibXoM0

ETHICAL CONCERNS OF SEARCHING FEMALE NEWCOMER'S EXPERIENCES: REFLECTIONS FROM THE FIELD

Fadi Hasan

Introduction

"Will the research make life even harder to cope with because sad memories and thoughts are revived? Is the researcher exploiting persons in a vulnerable position?" (Dyregrov et al., 2000). These fundamental questions indicate that conducting research on experiences of females with refugee background presents several serious challenges fraught with both ethical dilemmas and the possibility of potential harm to respondents (Bailey and Williams, 2018). The current literature is abundant with ethical guidelines. However, it often provides general guidance and is limited in specific practical contexts (Arifin, 2018).

This paper aims to present i) female newcomers' responses to participation in research and ii) practical ethical issues which may arise during research with female refugees. This paper is based on reflections from the empirical fieldwork of three papers, namely "Economic security among Syrian female refugees in Athens", "Asylum, Gender, and Home: The experiences of Syrian female refugees in Osnabrück/ Germany", and "Negotiations of Identity, Belonging and Feelings of Home among female Newcomers in Osnabrück". The research design and methods in all these works are qualitative research design, based on in-depth, face-to-face, and online interviews consisting of open-ended questions. All the previous papers were fielded and conducted by the researcher himself during the years 2019 and 2021. Germany and Greece are the research sites. The principal goal is to reflect on practical solutions to these challenges beyond what is being theoretically portrayed in the literature to ensure "zero-harm" research practices, where ethical responsibilities are realized.

Brief Review of the Literature

As a researcher, being sensitive to interviews means practicing intercultural competencies and cross-cultural skills. An interviewer who coordinates the conversation process and asks questions should be attentive to the general interviewing atmosphere. However, keeping and increasing cooperative participation and participants' corresponding attitude toward a different gender is the most daunting and challenging task for many researchers. Like any other communicative interaction, interviews always take place in a "gendered context" (Williams and Heikes, 1993), and many studies have shown that participants may exhibit different attitudes towards researchers of different genders (Kerr and MacCoun, 1985).

Put differently, gender often influences the interviewees' decision-making in taking part or refraining from taking part. Literature has shown that this is due, in part, to perceived asymmetries and power based on constructed differences and inequalities between males and females, forcing them to behave and adopt various attitudes (Parpart et al., 2000). Cigarini et al. (2020) and Molina et al. (2013) further explain that female interlocutors' cooperative behaviors and cooperation decisions depend on who the interviewer is. These studies concluded that females showed low cooperation rates when their interviewer is a man.

Summary of Findings

Though the literature would indicate gendered discrepancies in comfort levels, my empirical studies in Germany and Greece have found the opposite to be true. Most of the female participants were eager and comfortable talking about sensitive issues and experiences. From this standpoint, my research found that the female newcomers' status and position, coupled with the researcher's professionalism in demonstrating sensitivity and intercultural skills, contribute to generating their voluntary and positive reactions.

Furthermore, during the process of searching for potential participants, I find that willingness to accept or refuse of interviewing, in general, had been based on their social and religious positions. For example, in one case, one female expressed her great interest in participating. However, she pulled back because of her "doctrinal instructions". She stated that holding discussions about private religious ideologies outside the sect is a "taboo" even though it was made clear to her that the research scope does not include any religious orientations or involvement.

This finding corresponds with other literature which demonstrates that gender is not the sole factor that prompts or refrains participants from participating in studies (Leet-Pellegrini, 1980). For instance, Atkins and O' Barr (1980) concluded that females' social status influences their sense of cooperation and engagement in the research. The researcher's skills in understanding sensitivity and anticipating any potential difficulties and tensions which may serve as significant factors in preventing participation.

Recommendations

1. Sensitivity towards difficult topics

In the context of this research, female refugees may have been subjected to systematic human rights abuses including sexual violence. Thus, there is a need for mindfulness that participants might be vulnerable to any unsolicited memories or engage in one way or another (even indirectly) within stories, traumatic events, experiences, and opinions. Therefore, understanding sensibility while interviewing females with refugee background means anticipating any potential difficulties and tensions which may arise during the interview—such as emotional reactions, sadness, and embarrassment. Therefore, scholars should employ their best efforts to ensure that interview questions would not trigger any painful memories or interfere with events that participants did not want to share voluntarily. The latter point is exemplified by the following transcription extract:[1]

> *Fadi: What are the reasons that made you leave your country before 3 or 4 years?*
>
> *Fatima: There were political reasons, but if my words are going to be revealed, I would be in a risky situation. I am afraid to answer this question. (28.41)*
>
> *Fadi: No. Nothing is going to be revealed. However, I will not like to ask these questions to avoid any trouble.*
>
> *Fatima: This is a big political problem. So, I cannot talk about it.*
>
> *Fadi: Of course, you don't have to answer. We are going to avoid this question. (28.58)*

2. Creating a conducive environment for the interviewee

Besides the content of the interview, female interviewees should be informed and advised to choose a

---

[1] All interview transcripts should be provided with pseudonyms.

proper, safe, and secure place without access to any family members or outsiders, and a researcher should implement appropriate time and place considerations.

For example, before conducting the interviews, one should ensure that every female participant has selected a suitable time. Due to other commitments which are often gendered in nature, such as childcare, there may be a need to create additional considerations. Adjusting the academic fieldwork schedule to their time selection would therefore ensure that they feel comfortable without any pressure. In conducting my own interviews, for instance, I waited for two weeks for one interviewee whilst she was busy with family commitments. She explained that she understood the academic reasons for the interview, however, she thought that this may cause some problems with her mother-in-law who was visiting at the time. With another interviewee, I conducted the interview late at night once she had carried out her domestic responsibilities. A further reason for a postponement for another woman was due to religious prayers and devotions on Friday.

3. Pre-considering ethical norms for oneself as an interviewer

To a certain extent, participation in interviews may influence the lives of female participants. Before starting the process of conducting interviews, a researcher should make a clear and intentional decision to carry out the whole research in full adherence to ethical norms and considerations. The following practical solutions can prevent any ethical risks in research on female newcomers that can cause them any potentially harmful effects:

1.   Voluntary participation:

All respondents should participate in any study voluntarily. As a result, all interviews can be conducted after ensuring that participants were adequately informed about the study's purpose and the data collection process. For example, all potential participants should be provided with a summary of study information in both their mother language and research language, including research methods, aims, objectives, and a short biography. Then, they should be given the appropriate time around one week to decide whether to participate or decline. At the beginning of the interviews, all participants should be given an oral and clear explanation about their rights, including their voluntary participation; the possibility to withdraw from the study; to drop out of any question whenever they are feeling uncomfortable. Interviewees should be granted their free and voluntary permission to have the interviews audio-recorded orally and through a written consent form:

> *Fadi: I would like to inform you about your rights as a participant in this interview. First, you have absolutely the right not to answer any question, if you don't like to it or if you are not comfortable with that question. (01:05) Second, you can tell me at any point in time during the interview to stop if you are not feeling comfortable. The result of this research I will use in my master thesis and other papers related to this study, but without mentioning your real name. (1:35) I would like to inform you as well that you have absolutely the right to ask me any question. Moreover, you can ask me to send you a copy of my master thesis, if you would like to have a look upon it.*
>
> *Sara: (2:00) Okay! Do I have the right to read your work in the future?*
>
> *Fadi: Yeah! Exactly! You have the right. Of course, not right now, but when the study is finished. You can tell me, please send me a copy of your master thesis. You are a participant in this research and this is also one of your rights as a participant. I will make sure that this audio record – after I have your permission – will be stored and saved in a way that no one can have access to it. I want to ask you a question. I want to record this interview if you agree. If you say 'yes', I will record it, and if you say 'no' I will not. I want to record it because, later on, I need to write it down and save it into computer programs so that we can get codes and data, etc. Would you please allow me to record this*

interview?

> *Sara: Yes, I agree! (2:55)*

2. Language as a central tool:

Language is a crucial tool and constitutive force for females to articulate their personal experiences and provide rich details to grasp their social worldview, self and reality, and enabling them to feel confident and comfortable. Therefore, it should become a focus of attention to allow female participants to use their preferred language choice during the interviews if it is possible for the researcher. This cannot deny however the arduous and time-consuming endeavors with respect to translation and transcription.

3. Appropriate terminology and relations:

There is also a need to ensure care regarding language and terms used. Issues of real or potential harm to participants are further addressed in the ethical codes by advocating care over maintaining a sensitive approach to using the language and terms. Ethical issues related to offending participants' self-esteem, human indignity and or being deceived or being used as objects, should become a topic of concern. For example, the term "refugee" is used as a legal category to refer to people who successfully applied for asylum and have been granted refugee protection status (OCED, 2016). It is also a socially constructed category, which has multi-layered consequences and negative connotations. Therefore, at various stages of any research, in particular, in the information sheet, consent form, and during conducting the interviews, words "newcomers or forced migrants" are used synonymously. Words which used to humanize people who have been displaced from their homes but end up demonizing them instead should be carefully addressed.

4. Anonymity and Confidentiality:

Throughout all stages of the research cycle, high priority should be given to keeping participants' information confidential. First, researchers can have female participants' names and identity protected by using pseudonyms. The code names can be used without political, ethnic, or religious connotations such as "Nadia" and "Tawakkol". Second, in the write-up/analysis of the study, references to personal information can be omitted in quotations. To enhance anonymity, data can be stored in a safe and locked environment. For example, recordings and electronic data can be saved in encrypted devices and protected by using a password. Third, researchers can ensure that interviews are conducted individually and in a private and quiet place (using earphones, if virtual). As for the purpose of academic credibility, the transcripts can be shared with supervisors only through password-protected email. For example, "Fatima", a pen-name for an Egyptian refugee woman in Germany, mentioned during the course of the interview real names of her family members. Thereby required that references of the personal information to be deleted. This point is illustrated by the following interview excerpt:

> *Fatima: I smuggled my first child, then they threatened to harm my second child. I smuggled my son in 2015. I thought I would relax because I had smuggled my son. They threatened me saying that they would arrest (****) if I did not tell him where (****) was? My life was really full of terrors. It was too big for me to bear. I wondered whether my decision was right or wrong. I prayed to God: "If it was good, let it be, and if it was bad, let it not be." No one helped me in my decisions. No one encouraged me.*

Conclusion

In short, holding conversations with people is an effective method for collecting rich and detailed data. To produce comprehensive and sophisticated knowledge, scholars should position females as powerful experts and autobiographical narrators of their diverse voices and discourses. Simultaneously, they should be concerned about interviewees' reactions and emotions while sharing their stories, thoughts, experiences, feelings, and opinions. The ethical obligations of researchers should ensure that involvement in research will be positive and beneficial with zero potential harm to female participants.

References

Arifin, S. R. M. (2018). Ethical considerations in qualitative study. *International Journal of Care Scholars*, *1*(2), 30–33. https://doi.org/h74t

Atkins, B. K., & O'Barr, W. M. (1980). 'Women's Language'or 'Powerless Language'? *Language and Gender: A Reader*, 377–387. 10.1007/978-1-349-92299-4_11.

Bailey, L., & Williams, S. J. (2018). The ethical challenges of researching refugee education. *Qualitative Research Journal*, *18*(4), 359–370. https://doi.org/h23s

Cigarini, A., Vicens, J., & Perelló, J. (2020). Gender-based pairings influence cooperative expectations and behaviours. *Scientific Reports*, *10*(1), 1041. https://doi.org/gn4m8g

Parpart, J. L., Connelly, P., & Eudine Barriteau. (2000). *Theoretical perspectives on gender and development*. International Development Research Centre.

Dyregrov, K., Dyregrov, A., & Raundalen, M. (2000). Refugee families' experience of research participation. *Journal of Traumatic Stress*, *13*(3), 413–426. https://doi.org/b9wg6b

Kerr, N. L., & MacCoun, R. J. (1985). Role expectations in social dilemmas: Sex roles and task motivation in groups. *Journal of Personality and Social Psychology*, *49*(6), 1547–1556. https://doi.org/dfqr46

Leet-Pellegrini, H. M. (1980). Conversational dominance as a function of gender and expertise. In *Language* (pp. 97–104). Elsevier. https://doi.org/h74v

Molina, J. A., Giménez-Nadal, J. I., Cuesta, J. A., Gracia-Lazaro, C., Moreno, Y., & Sanchez, A. (2013). Gender Differences in Cooperation: Experimental Evidence on High School Students. *PLoS ONE*, *8*(12), e83700. https://doi.org/gn6gxb

OECD. (2016). *Making Integration Work: Refugees and others in need of protection*, Making Integration Work, OECD Publishing, Paris. https://doi.org/h74w

Williams, C. L., & Heikes, E. J. (1993). The importance of researcher's gender in the in-depth interview: Evidence from two case studies of male nurses. *Gender & Society*, *7*(2), 280–fe291. https://doi.org/d2cnbr

THE CHALLENGES OF PRODUCING MIGRATION-RELATED INFORMATION IN THE CONTEXT OF COVID-19 FROM A HUMAN RIGHTS APPROACH: THE CASE OF THE FIRST NATIONAL MIGRATION SURVEY IN ARGENTINA

Natalia Debandi[1]

Introduction

Argentina is a country with a long history of receiving migrants, but there is an important gap in the production of updated data on the situation and characteristics of this population. This article presents the National Migrant Survey of Argentina, a survey conducted from a practical human rights approach in 2020 during the Covid-19 pandemic.

Argentina comprises about 2.2 million migrants, positioning it as the country with the highest net number of migrants in Latin America. In comparison to the total population, the proportion of migrants is 4.9% (according to projections of ONU), a value that has increased slightly in the last two decades from 4.2% in 2001; nonetheless, this projected proportion is still far from 29.9% in 1914 (INDEC, 2011). The historical migration from Europe, mainly from Spain and Italy, was joined during the last century by regional border migration, mainly from Paraguay, Bolivia and Chile. In the last decades—in line with the current situation in the region—a diversification has taken place in terms of migration origin, incorporating Latin American countries such as Colombia, Peru, Cuba, Venezuela, and extra-regional countries such as Haiti, Senegal, China, and others.

On the other hand, Argentina was a pioneer both in Latin America and worldwide in renewing its migration policy in 2004 (Argentine Law 25.871), incorporating the right to migrate as a human right (García & Nejamkis, 2018). Argentine migration policy includes a number of universal guarantees for migrants, such as healthcare and education, regardless of their migration status. Despite these advances in the regulatory sphere, there are numerous studies and research papers reporting breaches in the actual access to these rights, resulting in the emergence of problems in several fields, such as access to healthcare, personal documentation, recourse to the law, regular education, and the persistence of discrimination, among many others (Ceriani, 2016; Penchaszadeh, Nicolao, & Debandi, 2022).

Although academic studies on international migration in Argentina are numerous and growing in number (Domenech & Pereira, 2017), but most of them are of a qualitative nature and, if quantitative, they focus on a particular nationality, e.g., Bolivians or Venezuelans. The main reason is the lack of good quality, up-to-date, official data sources. The National Census is the only survey providing comprehensive information on the migrant population, but it was last fielded in 2010 before several important transformations in migration flows of the last decade. The second representative statistics source is the Permanent Household Survey (Encuesta Permanente de Hogares or EPH), fielded only

[1] PhD in Social Sciences (UBA, Argentina - Paris IV, France). Researcher at the National University of Río Negro - Institute of Public Policy and Government, Argentina. Email: nataliadebandi@gmail.com.

at the level of the country´s urban nodes; therefore the EPH does not provide data for rural migration patterns. The only time a complementary survey was carried out was 2001 with the Complementary Survey on International Migrations (Encuesta Complementaria de Migraciones Internacionales or ECMI), which was fielded as part of the National Census on Population, Households and Housing of that same year.

The starting point of the National Migrant Survey

However, having further disaggregated data is particularly important in Argentina. Argentina, being a federal country, has policies that are heterogeneous by province. This produces a wide range of information systems that are often incompatible with each other and that i) fail to accurately record enough the variables associated to nationality and/or country of origin and ii) exhibit serious quality issues (Ribotta et al., 2019).

Thus, there has historically a lack of quantitative data available for academics, organizations, and activist groups, and even State agencies in charge of designing public policy for the migration population; nonetheless, this data scarcity became even more evident after the Covid-19 pandemic. When the Covid-19 pandemic began around March 2020, Argentina was in the midst of a deep economic crisis, with overwhelming poverty rates and severe hardship within the migrant population who, conditioned by restrictive and xenophobic policies implemented in the previous years, found it increasingly difficult to access documentation, healthcare or education (Debandi & Penchaszadeh, 2020; Gavazzo & Penchaszadeh, 2020). Mobility restrictions and strict border closure, along with the exclusion of a vast majority of the migrant population from social welfare policies and programs implemented in the first year of the pandemic, worsened the situation of many migrants even further. In this context, it became crucial to respond to the need for data that would produce reliable information and facilitate practicable policy.

Further, with the pandemic, there were greater opportunities and pressures for digital and technological changes that encouraged some groups to use devices who had not before. The pressing need for data and the virtualization of a great deal of social life promoted the development of the first National Migration Survey in Argentina (Encuesta Nacional Migrante de Argentina, or ENMA). This survey was carried out by the migration and shelter branch of the research group Red de investigaciones en Derechos Humanos, belonging to the Consejo Nacional de Investigaciones Científicas y Técnicas (CONICET), and called RIOSP-CONICET, with the participation, throughout all its stages, of a wide spectrum of social organization, activists and researchers.

Below, I briefly present three core aspects of the ENMA proposal—namely, the human rights approach, the collective construction and the methodological design.

Human Rights Approach and Collective Production of Knowledge

A human rights approach argues for the addressees of public policy to be positioned as subjects of rights, i.e., actors who can demand certain provisions and conducts from the State and of society (Abramovich & Pautassi, 2009). In addition, a human rights approach includes as founding principles, social participation and production of information. The rights-based approach seeks to move from a focus on assistance to placing the subject, in this case migrants, as bearers of their own life stories and rights vis-à-vis the State. However, one might ask, what is the meaning of producing information and knowledge on migrant populations from a human rights approach? And more specifically, in terms of methodology, what is the meaning of carrying out a survey from a human rights perspective?

Although this would require systematic development, the starting point in ENMA was the collective construction of information and knowledge: The basic principle was to consider that migrants were not—and are not, still—circumstantial or secondary participants at a given stage but rather active promoters and authors of such knowledge. In that sense, migrants were not only indispensable as driving forces for the project but also active participants—in equivalent conditions to researchers and academics—in the design of instruments (the survey), their dissemination, implementation and resulting analysis.

In the design of the questionnaire and the initial conceptual debates around it, there were 32 people involved; among them, there were researchers from the aforementioned Red de Derechos Humanos (RIOSP-CONICET), representatives of migrant groups and social organization advocates. In practical terms, the exchanges resulted in the inclusion in the questionnaire of the main interests of migrant communities, and the exclusion or some "classic" sociodemographic questions, affecting as well the ways in which certain were asked and framed. At the implementation stage, some new migrant organizations, which played a key role at making the questionnaire reach out to certain districts and provinces, were incorporated.

Methodological Design and Results

As previously mentioned, the pandemic made it particularly important for data collection and deepened the collaborative ties between academic and social organizations and made many people more acquainted with the use of digital communication technologies. In the case of ENMA, this was a key factor for its implementation. In the first place, due to costs, it would have been impossible for ENMA to be carried it out in a context of "normality" (without the conditions given by the pandemic, including mobility restriction). Secondly, a virtualization strategy for a survey such as this one would probably have never been effective in other circumstances, such as the previous to the pandemic, due to the lack of use of technology by the migrant population, among other factors.

The goal of ENMA was to obtain information on the access to rights (health, labor, education, housing, among others) of migrant population throughout the country. Along the same lines, ENMA aimed to obtain representative data for certain nationalities on which there was no updated information due to their being more recent, less numerous or less accessible, among them Venezuelans, Senegalese, Haitian, and Chinese. Based on these two propositions, a quota sampling design was developed, considering the following variables: nationality, age, gender, and place of residence during the last Census (2010), and the quotas were adjusted according to more recent data extracted from the Permanent Household Survey (2019). An initial scope of 2000 cases was stipulated, and it was later exceeded, obtaining 3114 valid responses, in which the aforementioned groups became overrepresented.

The survey was carried out by means of an online self-administered questionnaire, translated into three languages apart from Spanish (Haitian Creole, Wolof, and Chinese). It remained active for a month and a half. The distance to the quotas was monitored weekly, and specific strategies were developed for further dissemination of the questionnaire, mainly on social media and WhatsApp groups. In some cases, there were phone calls made by the migrant organizations in order to support migrants at completing the survey.

The first ENMA result to be published was the Statistical Migration Yearbook (Anuario Estadístico Migratorio: Debandi, Nicolao, and Penchaszadeh, 2021), also developed in a collaborative manner among different researchers and representatives of migrant groups. The data collected by ENMA, once tidied and adjusted (an example of this is ensuring all records remained anonymous) is available in an open format at the website of the aforementioned Red de derechos humanos. So far, data access has been requested by over 30 people (researchers and activists) or institutions (State organisms, international agencies and social organizations).

The ENMA data is currently the best up-to-date information on the situation of migrants in the country. It incorporated questions that had never been asked before, such as languages, ethnicity, difficulties in accessing health care and discrimination, among others. The ENMA is also proposed as a specific methodology, based on a rights-based approach. This methodological proposal seeks to promote research respecting the experience and knowledge of migrants themselves as subjects of rights.

References

Abramovich, V. & Pautassi, L. (2009). "El enfoque de derechos y la institucionalidad de las políticas sociales" (*Rights Approach and Social Policy Intitutionality*). In: Abramovich, V., & Pautassi, L. (Comps): La revisión judicial de las políticas sociales. Case Study, Buenos Aires, Del Puerto.

Ceriani Cernadas, P. (2016). Ampliación de derechos en tiempos de crisis: la política migratoria en Argentina desde 2003. (*Expansion of Rights at Times of Crisis: Migratory Policy in Argentina Since 2003*). Red Universitaria sobre Derechos Humanos y Democratización para América Latina, 5 (8): 14-47.

Debandi, N., Nicolao, J & Penchaszadeh, A. P. (Coords.) (2021) Anuario Estadístico Migratorio de la Argentina 2020 (*Statistical Migration Yearbook of Argentina*). Buenos Aires: CONICET.

Debandi, N & Penchaszadeh, A. P. (2020) Ser migrante en tiempos de pandemia (*Being a Migrant During the Times of the Pandemic*). Revista Ciencia Hoy, v. 29, no. 172, pp. 33-37.

Domenech, E. & Pereira, A. (2017). Estudios migratorios e investigación académica sobre las políticas de migraciones internacionales en Argentina. Migraciones internacionales en América Latina: miradas críticas a la producción de un campo de conocimientos (*Migration Studies and Academic Research on International Migration Policies in Argentina. International Migrations in Latin America: Critical Views to the Production of a Field of Knowlege*), Íconos 58.

García, L. & Nejamkis, L. (2018). Regulación migratoria en la Argentina actual: del "modelo" regional al recorte de derechos. (*Migration Regulation in Current Argentina: from the Regional "Model" to the Reduction of Rights*). Revista de Ciencias Sociales e Historia; Vol. II, No 2.

Gavazzo, N. & Penchaszadeh, A. P. (2020) La otra pandemia. Migrantes entre el olvido estatal y el apoyo de las redes comunitarias. (*The other pandemic. Migrants Between State Oblivion and Support from Communal Networks*). In: DIAZ, María (Coord.). (Trans)fronteriza: Pandemia y Migración, Buenos Aires: CLACSO, pp. 47-56.

INDEC- Instituto Nacional de Estadística y Censo (2011). Censo Nacional de Población, Hogares y Viviendas 2010 (*National Census on Population, Households and Housing 2010*). Data Analysis. Final Results.

Penchaszadeh, A. P. (2021). De papeles y derechos. La difícil traducción del paradigma de derechos humanos en la política migratoria de la Argentina actual. (*On Papers and Rights. The Difficult Translation of the Paradigm of Human Rights in Argentina's Current Migration Policies*). Colombia Internacional, No. 106, pp. 3-27.

Penchaszadeh, A. P., Nicolao, J., and Debandi, N. (2022). Impacto de la pandemia y sus medidas asociadas sobre la población migrante en Argentina (*Impact of the Pandemic and its Measures on the Migrant Population in Argentina*, Si Somos Americanos. Revista de Estudios Transfronterizos, 22(1), 90-113

Ribotta, B., Santillán Pizarro, M. M., & González, L. M. (2018). ¿Cómo, cuánto y por qué? Sobre el ejercicio de derechos en poblaciones en situaciones de vulnerabilidad social, una primera aproximación al potencial y limitaciones de las fuentes de datos sociodemográficos. (*How, How many or how much and Why? On the Exercise of Rights in Vulnerable Situation Populations, A First Approach to the Potentialities and Limitations of the Sources of Sociodemographic Data*). In: Ejercicio de derechos y poblaciones en situación de vulnerabilidad social. ¿Qué nos dicen las fuentes de datos en Argentina? (1994-2005). Córdoba (Argentina): CEPYD-CIECS CONICET.

THE POWER OF CATEGORIZATION: REFLECTIONS ON UNHCR'S CATEGORY OF 'VENEZUELANS DISPLACED ABROAD'

Luisa Feline Freier[1]

The Venezuelan exodus is the second biggest displacement scenario in the world and meets three out of the five elements of the refugee definition of the regional 1984 Cartagena Declaration, which most countries in the region have incorporated into their national legislation. However, numbers of both Venezuelan asylum seekers and recognized refugees remain extremely low. In this context, the UNHCR created the category 'Venezuelans displaced abroad', which was first introduced in its 2019 Global Trends Report. Acknowledging the large percentage of Venezuelans who remain outside of the asylum system, the UNHCR maintains that this group is entitled to international protection. However, they are not officially counted as asylum seekers, refugees or 'others of concern to the UNHCR'. Based on 16 elite interviews this research explores the following questions: How has the category of 'Venezuelans displaced abroad' affected the sense- and decision-making of both representatives of international organizations and policy makers, and in how far did the category shape Peru's policy reactions to Venezuelan displacement?

Introduction

In the past decades, Migration Studies have gained increasing academic and socio-political recognition and importance. In this context, scholars began paying attention to how knowledge on migration is produced by researchers, (non)-governmental actors, and the media (Amelina, 2021; Nieswand & Drotbohm, 2014). The reflexive turn in Migration Studies seeks to understand which migration-related categories, narratives, and data are produced and used by actors including politicians, international organizations, and academics, why and to which effect. It thus seeks to unpack the power of categorization (see Imiscoe, 2022). Intriguingly, the reflexive turn in Migration Studies mirrors the South-North bias in the migration literature more broadly, in that such studies have focused on critical epistemological approaches to migration phenomena in the Global North. We argue that is necessary to conceptualize the production of knowledge on migration as a situated, context-dependent process across different geographical levels, recognizing global power structures.

Venezuelan displacement provides a compelling case for the study of categorization. First, in South America legislative reforms and the management of human mobility, including refugee protection, have centered on the protection and respect of migrants' human rights and expansive refugee definitions. The UNHCR even considers Latin American countries to be at the forefront of international refugee protection (Freier & Gauci 2020). Second, Venezuelans' plight meets three out of the five elements of the regional Cartagena definition of refugee (Freier, Berganza, and Blouin 2020). However, in the context of the Venezuelan exodus, governments in the region developed *ad hoc* policy responses, which are reflected - and were likely shaped - by UNHCR's creation of the category 'Venezuelans displaced abroad'. Third, UN organizations such as IOM and UNHCR have had a strong influence on the governance of Venezuelan displacement.

---

[1] Associate Professor and IDRC Chair on Forced Displacement, Universidad del Pacífico (Lima, Peru)

Background: Venezuelan Displacement, Policies and Categorization

With more than 7 million Venezuelans having left their homes in recent years, the Venezuelan displacement crisis is the largest exodus in Latin America's recent history and the second biggest displacement crisis in the world. The Covid-19 pandemic and the fuel crisis have aggravated the economic despair that Venezuelans experienced for years, creating a shortage of basic goods and one of the most severe hyperinflation scenarios in the world. In addition to the lack of food and medicine, and crumbling social services, people are leaving Venezuela because of widespread violence and insecurity, and for fear of being targeted based on their political opinions. Venezuelan displacement thus meets three out of the five elements of the regional Cartagena definition of refugee: massive violation of human rights, generalized violence and events that seriously disturb public order (Freier, Berganza, and Blouin 2020)

However, although fifteen countries in Latin America adopted the Cartagena definition into their domestic laws and leading bureaucrats in the region's refugee agencies are aware of the applicability of the Cartagena definition of refugee, only Brazil and Mexico have applied this definition to a significant number of Venezuelan citizens (ibid.). Many host countries developed *ad hoc* policy responses that have been highly dependent on the number of Venezuelan immigrants and refugees present in each country. With increasing numbers and rising xenophobia, the region's initial generosity shifted towards restrictive policy reactions and de facto border closures towards Venezuelans (Freier & Doña-Reveco, 2022).

This dilemma is reflected in the UNHCR's creation of the new category 'Venezuelans displaced abroad', which was first introduced in its 2019 Global Trends Report. Acknowledging the large percentage of Venezuelans who stay in their host countries, but remain outside of the asylum system, the UNHCR maintains that 'Venezuelans displaced abroad' are entitled to international protection considerations under the criteria contained in the Cartagena Declaration and should therefore be included in the global forced displacement total. However, they are not officially counted as asylum seekers, refugees or 'others of concern to the UNHCR', the traditional UNHCR label. Figure 1 shows the scale of Venezuelan displacement in relation to numbers of asylum seekers and refugees.

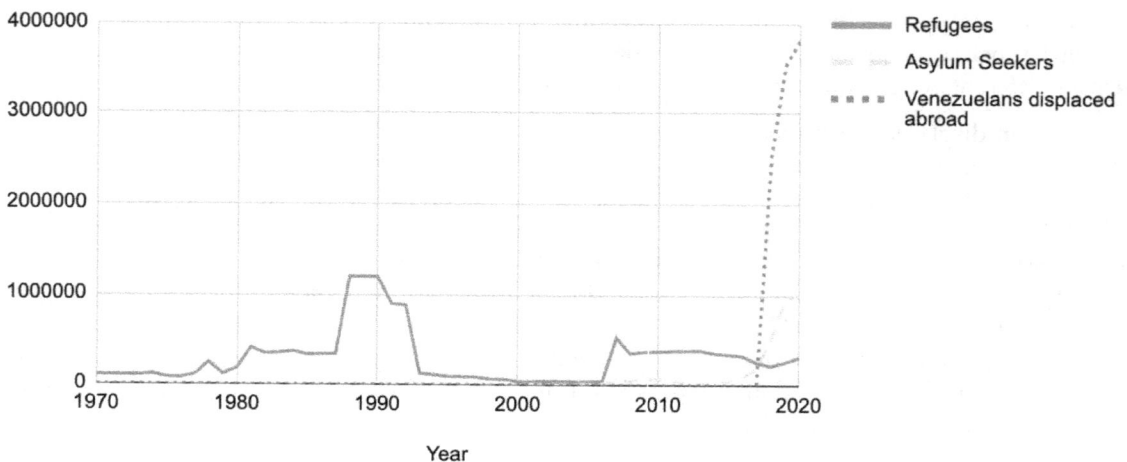

Refugees, Asylum Seekers and Venezuelans Displaced Abroad (1970-2020)

Source: UNHCR data, author elaboration

While the huge uptake in migrants can help explain the collapse of some of the region's asylum systems, there are other reasons for the lack of recognition of Venezuelans as refugees, including the lack of self-identification as such. Worldwide a relatively small number of Venezuelans have filed asylum applications, partly due to lacking information about the Cartagena refugee definition and its applicability to their situation (Freier and Bird 2021). This lack of information goes back to the fact that receiving states do not treat and inform Venezuelans as potential asylum seekers. In the context, this research asks how the category of 'Venezuelans displaced abroad' affected policy choices, including the tendency to treat Venezuelan displacement as a migration rather than an international protection scenario.

Case selection and Methodology

Peru is the largest recipient of Venezuelan asylum seekers world-wide, but the government treats them essentially as migrants. The state response to Venezuelan displacement has gone through three phases: openness under former president Pedro Pablo Kuczynski (July 2016–March 2018), growing restrictiveness under president Martín Vizcarra (March 2018 - November 2020), and technically led attempts to regularize the population (since early 2021). Initially, Peru made significant advances in providing Venezuelans the necessary documentation to work. Although Peru did not apply the Cartagena refugee definition or the Southern Common Market (Mercosur) Residence Agreement to a significant number of Venezuelans (Acosta et al. 2019), it was the first country in the region to create a special residence permit for Venezuelan migrants: the Temporary Residence Permit (PTP), which was launched in early 2017, renewed four times, and allowed Venezuelans to reside and work in Peru legally for one year. With the introduction of entry and residence requirements, asylum applications by Venezuelan nationals exploded, and soon made up the lion share of Venezuelan asylum claims worldwide. However, especially in the context of COVID-19 applications were barely processed (Castro & Freier, 2021). In mid 2021, there were over 530,000 asylum seekers in Peru but only 3,229 recognized refugees.

In this study we seek to explore, in how far the category 'Venezuelans displaced abroad' affected the sense- and decision-making of both representatives of international organizations and policy makers, and shaped policy options. Methodologically, the paper rests on 16 elite interviews with representatives of IOM, UNHCR, other IOs, NGOs and government officials working in Peruvian migration governance, guided by the following questions:

A. What does the category 'Venezuelans displaced abroad' entail for you?

B. Does the category 'Venezuelans displaced abroad' apply primarily to migrants or refugees?

C. How is the category 'Venezuelans displaced abroad' used in your work environment?

D. How is the category 'Venezuelans displaced abroad' used in migration governance?

E. What has been the impact of the category 'Venezuelans displaced abroad'?

F. In your opinion, what would have been the impact of using another category, such as 'refugees' or 'persons of concern to UNHCR'?

Initial results

A high ranking UNHCR official explained that the category 'Venezuelans displaced abroad' is a category agreed on between UNHCR and IOM to avoid tensions about institutional mandates and who should take the lead in the international response.

Although both state representatives and the IO/NGO sector recognize the term, state representatives found it more difficult to define. The latter group focused on the reasons for leaving Venezuela and the forced nature of the displacement. Conversely, state representatives tended to see the term as covering 'migrants' rather than 'refugees'. In contrast, representatives of IOs and NGOs saw an emphasis on 'refugees'. Intriguingly, this impression was even shared by an IOM representative.

Interviewees across the state and organizations agreed that the term 'Venezuelans displaced abroad' was not used in their work environment, and its use was limited to the formal UN environment. Public sector actors prefer the terms 'migrants', and in specific cases, 'refugees'. On the other hand, representatives of IOs and NGOs prefer the term 'refugees & migrants'.

Representatives of IOs and NGOs believe that the term creates confusion in the categorization and prevents various Venezuelans from recognizing their situation of vulnerability, and as such, requesting protection. Relatedly, both state and IO/NGO representatives agree that a positive impact would have been generated if another category was used instead of 'Venezuelans displaced abroad', specifically calling them 'refugees' as this category recognizes their rights and helps in negotiations between the state and IOs such as UNHCR.

In sum, our findings suggest that 'Venezuelans displaced abroad' is a category that is little used and not unequivocally understood and interpreted by stakeholders, thus leading to conceptual fuzziness. Stakeholders agree that the category has limited international and normative pressure on the Peruvian state to recognize Venezuelans as refugees and might have prevented displaced people themselves from identifying as refugees themselves. These preliminary results suggest that the category expanded Peru's policy options to treat Venezuelans as migrants rather than refugees and thus limited their protection.

References

Acosta, D., C. Blouin and L.F. Freier (2019) "La emigracion venezolana: respuestas latinoamericanas", Documento de Trabajo, no 3 (2ªepoca). Fundacion Carolina, Madrid.

Amelina, A. (2021). After the reflexive turn in migration studies: Towards the doing migration approach. *Population, space and place, 27*(1), https://onlinelibrary.wiley.com/doi/full/10.1002/psp.2368.

Blouin, C., Berganza, I., & Freier, L. F. (2020). The spirit of Cartagena? Applying the extended refugee definition to Venezuelans in Latin America. *Forced Migration Review, 63,* 64-66.

Duplan, K., & Cranston, S. (2022). A reflexive perspective on privileged migration studies: what's the point?. *Blog series of the IMISCOE Standing Committee'Reflexivities in Migration Studies' and the nccr-on the move.*

Freier, L. F., Berganza, I., & Blouin, C. (2022). The Cartagena Refugee Definition and Venezuelan Displacement in Latin America 1. *International Migration, 60*(1), 18-36.

Freier, L. F., Bird, M., Brauckmeyer, G., Kvietok, A., Licheri, D., Román, E. L., ... & Ponce, L. (2021). Estudio de opinión sobre la población extranjera en el Perú.

Freier, L. F., & Brauckmeyer, G. (2020). Migrantes venezolanos y COVID-19: impacto de la cuarentena y propuestas para la apertura. *Por una nueva convivencia. La sociedad peruana en tiempos de COVID-19: escenarios, propuestas de política y acción pública.*

Freier, L.F. & Doña-Reveco, C. (2022). "Latin American Political and Policy Responses to Venezuelan Displacement: Introduction to the Special Issue." International Migration.

Freier, L. F., & Gauci, J. P. (2020). Refugee Rights Across Regions: A comparative overview of legislative good practices in Latin America and the EU. *Refugee Survey Quarterly, 39*(3), 321-362. https://academic.oup.com/rsq/article/39/3/321/5918923

Freier, L. F., Luzes, M., Lyra Jubilut, L., Vera Espinoza, M., & Mezzanotti, G. (2020). Latin America and Refugee Protection: Regimes, Logics and Challenges.

Luzes, M., Freier, L. F., Castro, M., & Brauckmeyer, G. (2021). Inmigración venezolana en Perú. Regularización migratoria y sistemas de refugio. *Equilibrium CenDE,* 257-274.

Nieswand, B., & Drotbohm, H. (2014). Einleitung: Die reflexive Wende in der Migrationsforschung. In *Kultur, Gesellschaft, Migration.* (pp. 1-37). Springer VS, Wiesbaden. https://link.springer.com/chapter/10.1007/978-3-658-03626-3_1.

MIGRATION DATA: EVIDENCE FOR MAKING REINTEGRATION POLICY IN NEPAL

Anurag Devkota[1]

Nepal Labour Migration Profile

Nepal has emerged as one of the most prominent countries of origin for foreign labor where "an average of 1,500 Nepalese migrant workers officially leave Nepal every day for foreign employment" (UN Human Rights Council, 2019). This number is significantly larger when considering the high levels of migration from Nepal through unofficial channels. The Department of Foreign Employment (DoFE) reports that a total of 190,453 new labour permits were issued to Nepali migrant workers for foreign employment in countries other than India between 2019 and 2020.[2] The number of labour permits were reduced to 72,081 (7,178 women and 64,903 men) between 2020 to 2021, following the COVID-19 pandemic (Department of Foreign Employment, 2021). However, recently the country has witnessed an exponential rise in foreign labour migration, where 55,523[3] migrant workers from Nepal obtained a labour permit in just one month, between March and April of 2022 (Department of Foreign Employment, 2022).

The Government of Nepal has approved 110 countries as labour destinations, where Qatar, Malaysia, Saudi Arabia, the United Arab Emirates (UAE) and Kuwait are the five most popular destinations among Nepali labour migrants outside of India comprising over 90 percent of total migrant workers (MoLESS, 2020). According to the Migration in Nepal report, there are an estimated 500,000 Nepali migrants in Malaysia, the most popular labour destination (aside from India), followed by Qatar with over 400,000, Saudi Arabia with 334,451, the United Arab of Emirates with 224,905 and Kuwait with 70,000 (MoLESS, 2020). This sharp increase in foreign labour migration has substantially contributed to the economy of the nation. Remittances from Nepali migrant workers have been a stable source of income for Nepal, currently accounting for 24.1 percent of the country's GDP (The World Bank, 2020). In 2019, Nepal was the fifth highest in terms of ratio of remittances to GDP in the world (ADB, 2022). It is estimated that over 56 percent of Nepali households rely on remittances, which has largely contributed to significant alleviation of poverty, malnutrition, and hunger in Nepal (Joshi, S. et. al., 2020).

Covid 19 Pandemic, Return Migration and Reintegration Policy Needs

With the era of immobility exacerbated by the Covid 19 pandemic, the country came to witness the conversion in the patterns of migration. Reverse migration exposed the migrant workers (especially in the global south) to distinct vulnerabilities of "finding themselves home". For instance, hundreds of returnee Nepali migrant workers who struggled to return home in the first instance were forced to

---

[1] Human Rights Lawyer, Law and Policy Forum for Social Justice. aba.anurag@gmail.com.
[2] The number indicates of the new approval (without re-entry) from July 2019 to June 2020
[3] Total with Re-entry permits

remigrate. The recent data of obtaining the labour approval for foreign employment has been a record high, in past two months more than 1,800 migrant workers left the country on a daily basis. The scale of foreign labour migration that the country has come to witness especially after the COVID-19 pandemic has been alarming and largely associated with the absence of the timely and evidence-based reintegration frameworks and employment policies. The unfortunate consequences of the inactions demonstrated by the policy makers towards the importance of disaggregated data on the stocks of returnee migrants, the data on gender, skills, sector of employment among others, has led to the weaker with weaker frameworks, and implementation as a lackluster. The vulnerabilities of undocumented and India-bound migrant workers need a special mention as they are often excluded from the official data of the Government of Nepal (considering the open border agreement between the two), followed with the exclusion on the schemes and welfare packages after return.

The policy frameworks on addressing the social and economic challenges of reintegration at the domestic level has been the urgent need of the time, while the lack of data on the same has been an impediment in addressing this. Although, the government of Nepal bears an accountability to develop evidence-based policy arrangements through the collection and harmonization of accurate and disaggregated data, by virtue of being a champion country to Global Compact on Migration (GCM), the efficacy in translating the commitment into practice was challenged with the glaring contradictions, signifying the importance of policy implications of measuring migration. The data profiling of the government at its present status has not been utilized in its fullest efficacy to evidence the policy making process in Nepal. The lack of disaggregated data on gender, skills, occupations, geographic locations including the indicator to measure the status of the returnee migration worker in the overall migration cycle has hampered the overall policy making process in Nepal.

Current Normative Frameworks

Precisely on reintegration, some notable references towards return and reintegration are being considered on the governing policies of Nepal. For instance, the approach paper of the fifteenth five-year plan of National Planning Commission (fiscal year 2019-20 to 2023-24) of Nepal aims towards establishing and maintaining digital records of the skills of returnee migrant workers in order to attract foreign direct investment more efficiently (National Planning Commission, 2019). Similarly, the National Strategic Action Plan (2015-20) of the Ministry of Labour, Employment and Social Security (MoLESS) envisions socio-economic reintegration of returned workers and utilizing the experiences of returnee migrant workers in activities and programs related to the socio-economic reintegration of Nepali migrant workers. The effectiveness of this has been challenged on the ground that no policy as such were executed during the period. The Local Governance Operations Act, 2017 further mandates local governments with the responsibility to collect and manage information and data of returnee migrant workers and design the social reintegration of the returnee migrant workers by utilizing the knowledge, skills and entrepreneurship gained from foreign employment (*Local Government Operation Act, 2017).*

However, the overall assessment of Nepal's migration governance framework finds that the governing policies framework are flawed and unfounded. Studies have suggested that the indicators of migration governance, including the internationally accepted principles and standards of labor migration, do not seem to be reflected anywhere in the normative and governance mechanism of the country (International Labour Organization, 2021). For example, the available policy frameworks do not proportionately reflect the detailed data based on gender, migration status, region, occupation and skills, while an integrated and comprehensive policy vis-a-vis the reintegration of returnee migrant workers is crucially absent from the governance framework. Hence, the current effort should align towards generating and managing the data in the first place. The reintegration policies and mechanisms that the country is currently trying to come out with, without due consideration to the disaggregated data on stocks, gender, skill, age, employment, geographic locations, status of migration including their social security/protection, is unfounded and indicates ineffective implementations. The upcoming policy should be based on up-to-date and reliable data and evidence in order to address unique challenges across different migration corridors, countries, regions and actors. The policy should be able to cater to the needs and vulnerabilities of returning migrant workers followed with targeted re-integration programmes including that of skills matching and registration, economic incentives, social protection for migrant workers, and/or psycho-social counseling, among other requirements.

International good practices and lessons for Nepal

The good practices of other countries vis-à-vis policy and structural arrangements regarding the reintegration of returning migrant workers could complement well in coming up with a strong reintegration mechanism for Nepal. For instance, close neighbors like the Philippines, Sri Lanka, and Vietnam, including the practices from Bangladesh, could be assessed, and learned from. The Migrant Workers and Overseas Filipinos Act of 1995of Philippines contains elaborated provisions on the return, repatriation and reintegration of migrant workers, and envisages for the National Reintegration Center for OFWs to be established under the Philippine Department of Labor and Employment, with an aim to provide counseling services to workers, wage employment assistance, skill training, and capacity building, and assistance to Filipino workers (Section 17, Migrant Workers and Overseas Filipinos Act, 1995, Philippines). The model serves to be an example towards the development of a re-integration and monitoring system at the government level. Similarly, in Vietnam, the Department of Labor has also set up a separate Law on Employment Support, targeting migrant workers returning from abroad. It seems that policy and structural arrangements have been made in this program to inform the migrant workers returning from abroad about the employment opportunities available to them and to give instructions on how to register for a job search. Similarly, encouraging migrant workers returning from abroad to work for themselves, as well as creating an environment conducive to self-employment and encouraging these workers to benefit not only themselves, but also prospective returnee migrant workers. Likewise, Bangladesh has very recently, with the assistance of IOM, developed a digital platform aiming towards improving the migration data management and evidence-based reintegration support programs (International Organisation on Migration, 2021).

The practicalities of measuring migration

The country requires a framework to explore the mechanisms to register the human and social capital, such as skills, and explore financial avenues to create investment opportunities for returnee migrant workers. It is critical to recognize the importance of developing platforms to create jobs, register skills, and create subsidies, loans, or other investment opportunities to create jobs that match the skills. At the same time, special packages, and mechanisms to house the social, cultural as well as psychological needs of the returnee migrant workers should be considered.

The Foreign Employment Information Management System (FEIMS), the digital platform recently launched by the Ministry of Labor, Employment, and Social Security, to keep records of the incoming and outgoing migrant workers could be well utilized in managing the database of the returnees including their skills, capital, and experiences. Similarly, linking the FEIMS with the Prime Minister's Employment Program (PMEP)[4] to link the skills and capitals of returnee migrants and the job

---

[4] A national flagship programme that guarantees the constitutional rights of employment to registered unemployed, official website: https://pmep.gov.np

matchings at the domestic level should be duly considered. In this way, the returning workers under the listed category would be prioritized based on their specific individual needs ranging from psycho-social support to financial advice or loan facilities. The pattern of return migration in lieu of the migration cycle needs a special focus considering specific individual needs and requirements.

The government could do well in terms of job matching as well as creating employment opportunities back home if the current priority is centralized towards establishing a strong data- and evidence-based policies followed with strong implementation and monitoring mechanisms. Social dialogues followed with engagements with non-state partners, including that of private agencies, serve as further evidence for an informed policy debate and policy reformations. The forthcoming policy frameworks should as well envision a mechanism to establish data vis-à-vis the domestic labour markets needs and potential employment areas for the returnee migrant workers. For instance, the current available data of the government finds that a large number of Nepali migrants are employed in sectors such as construction and agriculture in GCC countries, whilst at home the government is mobilizing huge projects on infrastructure building (national pride projects) and introducing revolutionary farming in Nepal. In the absence of robust and evidence-based policy and structural mechanisms, the returnee migrant workers have not been able to fit into the current priorities of the government. As such, a well-founded reintegration policy backed up with data and evidence has been the current need, indicating that in order for a policy framework to be strongly implemented at the ground level, the migration needs to be 'measured'. "Data is the Key".

References

Department of Foreign Employment. (2021). (rep.). *Country wise Labour Approval (without re-entry) for FY 2077/78*. Department of Foreign Employment. Retrieved August 14, 2022, from https://dofe.gov.np/yearly.aspx.

Department of Foreign Employment (DoFE). (2022, May 23). *Monthly Progress Report, May, 2022*. Department of Foreign Employment. Retrieved August 14, 2022. https://dofe.gov.np/monthly.aspx

International Labour Organization. (2021). *Recruitment of migrant workers from Nepal: Country profile*. International Labour Organization. https://www.ilo.org/wcmsp5/groups/public/---ed_norm/---ipec/documents/publication/wcms_814432.pdf

IOM Bangladesh. (2021, February 15). *First-ever digital data platform for improved reintegration of returning migrants*. IOM Bangladesh. https://bangladesh.iom.int/news/first-ever-digital-data-platform-improved-reintegration-returning-migrants

Joshi, S., Chhetri, N. S., Neupane, K., Dhakal, K. R., & Migration Lab. (2020). Rapid Assessment of Nepali Migrant Workers' Situation in Major Destination Countries During the COVID-19 Pandemic. *Nepal Policy Institute*. https://nepalpolicyinstitute.org/wp-content/uploads/2020/07/Migration-Situation_GCC-Malaysia-and-India_July-2020_Final-Version.pdf

Khadka, M. S., Nakarmi, N., & Thapa, M. K. C. (2022). Nepal Macroeconomic Update, April 2022. *Nepal Resident Mission (NRM) Macroeconomic Update, 10*(1).

Local Government Operation Act 2017, s. 11.2.1 (Npl.).

Migrant Workers and Overseas Filipinos Act 1995, (Ph)

Ministry of Labour, Employment and Social Security. (2020). *Nepal Labour Migration Report 2020*. Ministry of Labour, Employment and Social Security. https://moless.gov.np/wp-content/uploads/2020/03/Migration-Report-2020-English.pdf

National Planning Commission. (2020, March). *The Fifteenth Plan (Fiscal Year 2019/20 – 2023/24)*. National Planning Commission. https://npc.gov.np/images/category/15th_plan_English_Version.pdf

The United Nations Secretariat. (2018, April 30). *A/HRC/38/41/add.1: Report of the special rapporteur on the human rights of migrants on his mission to Nepal from 29 January to 5 February 2018*. The Office of the High Commissioner for Human Rights. https://www.ohchr.org/en/documents/country-reports/ahrc3841add1-report-special-rapporteur-human-rights-migrants-his-mission

The World Bank. (2020). Personal remittances, Received (% of GDP) - Nepal. https://data.worldbank.org/indicator/BX.TRF.PWKR.DT.GD.ZS?locations=NP

MAPPING POLICYMAKER PERSPECTIVES OF THE CLIMATE SECURITY-MIGRATION NEXUS IN NIGERIA: A SOCIAL MEDIA ANALYSIS

Bia Carneiro[1], Tanaya Dutta Gupta[2], Giuliano Resce[3], Peter Läderach[4], and Grazia Pacillo[5]

Introduction

Despite growing attention around the climate security-migration nexus, the linkages between climate change, migration, and conflict and security risks have remained a matter of debate for research, policy, and practice (Brzoska & Fröhlich, 2016; Boas et al., 2019). Attempts at gathering empirical evidence on this nexus (Abel et al., 2019), as well as global level policy instruments (IOM, 2018), have mainly focused on international contexts. At national and sub-national scales, interest and awareness around this nexus (von Uexkull & Buhaug, 2021; IPCC 2022) has yet to be reflected in the policy arena. Not only are the development of policies for national and human security and for climate adaptation and mitigation often detached, they largely fail to consider the complex pathways that connect these two dimensions with human mobility and immobility.

To address this gap, we apply an online issue mapping approach (Rogers et al, 2015) to assess representations of migration as a topic of governance within the public discourse of state actors related to climate security domains, using Nigeria as a case study. Not only is Sub-Saharan Africa a major climate migration hotspot, but Nigeria is one of the most vulnerable countries to slow-onset climate impacts, with up to 9.4 million people moving by 2050. Nigeria is also ranked among the countries with the most conflict-induced displaced people by 2020 (IDMC 2021, Rigaud et al., 2021).

As a country with medium exposure to ecological threats, Nigeria experiences climate-related fragility and mobility dynamics, in addition to developmental challenges due to COVID-induced shocks on its oil-dependent economy, and security risks due to violence between multiple actors, including Boko Haram, vigilante groups, security forces, and between ethnic groups over control of resources (World Bank 2021, Dorff et al. 2020).

This study investigates two research questions: 1) How is the climate security-migration nexus represented in Nigeria's policy agenda? 2) What associations between migration and other climate security variables are represented in the public discourse of policymakers?

In line with recent trends in academic research that use social media platforms as proxies for wider public discourse and engagement, this study relies on the foundations of Digital Methods (Rogers,

[1] Social Research & Media Specialist, CGIAR FOCUS Climate Security, Alliance of Bioversity International and CIAT. b.carneiro@cgiar.org
[2] Climate Action Specialist, CGIAR FOCUS Climate Security, Alliance of Bioversity International and CIAT. t.duttagupta@cgiar.org
[3] Senior Lecturer, Department of Economics, University of Molise.
[4] Senior Scientist, Senior Economist, CGIAR FOCUS Climate Security, Alliance of Bioversity International and CIAT.
[5] Lead Climate Security, CGIAR FOCUS Climate Security, Alliance of Bioversity International and CIAT.
Acknowledgements: This work was carried out with support from the CGIAR Initiative on Climate Resilience, ClimBeR. We would like to thank all funders who supported this research through their contributions to the CGIAR Trust Fund: https://www.cgiar.org/funders/.

2013; Carneiro et al, 2022) to explore the salience of the climate security-migration nexus among Nigerian policy actors at national level.

Methods and data

Twitter is widely recognised as an important digital forum, not only for information exchanges and dialogue at the personal level (Pearce et al, 2019), but also as a central venue for institutional communications. State leaders and government agencies have embraced social media as a space to connect with both constituents and international actors (Barberá and Zeitoff, 2018; Bertot et al, 2012), and news media increasingly rely on the platform as a primary source for official statements and position-taking. As a real-time, topic-driven platform, it enables detecting evolving trends and dynamics in public discourse (McDonald, 2013).

To frame perceptions around the climate security-migration nexus at the policy level in Nigeria, an analysis of government communications on Twitter was performed. Official, public profiles of state actors that engage with climate security issues were identified, including central government, ministries of agriculture, natural resources, the environment, and national security bodies. An algorithm was developed to extract all publicly available Tweets from these accounts (Table 1), with a total of 64,300 tweets collected between 2012-01-24 to 2021-08-04. Figure 1 shows a timeline of the Twitter activity by Nigerian state actors. Increased presence is noted from 2016-onwards.

Table 1. Official, public Twitter profiles of state actors selected for analysis.

Twitter profiles	No. Tweets
Federal Government	12256
House of Representatives	9792
President Muhammadu Buhari	3167
Presidency	9463
Ministry of Agriculture and Rural Development	3170
Department of Climate Change	564
Environment Ministry	4056
Ministry of Petroleum Resources	2557
Ministry of Power	519
Ministry of Water Resources	1235
Armed Forces of Nigeria	3036
Nigerian Army	3629
Ministry of Interior	2331
Police Force	8525

A scoping review (Dutta Gupta et al., 2021) on the climate security nexus in Nigeria – in which migration was highlighted as a key dimension – identified 44 key concepts covering conflict, climate, agricultural production, resources, and political and socioeconomic insecurities. From these, a custom taxonomy, to be detected in the corpus of tweets, was created using the term expansion strategy proposed in Carneiro et al (2022). A custom algorithm was developed to classify the text of the tweets, and topics were assessed through correlation measures to identify interlinkages.

Figure 1. Frequency of tweets over time

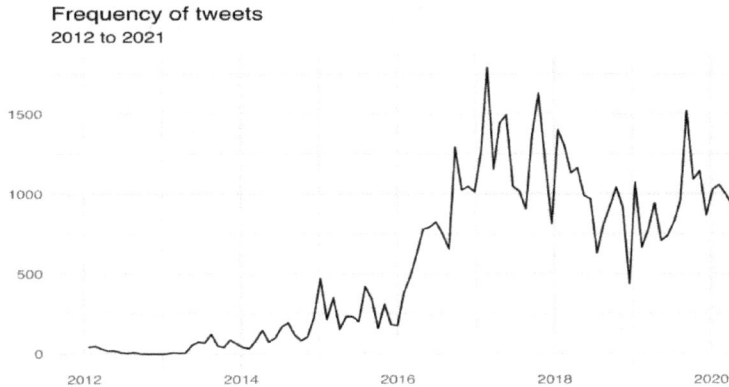

Frequency of tweets
2012 to 2021

Results

As a first approximation of themes covered by Nigerian climate security actors in their Twitter conversations, Figure 2 shows a word cloud for the 100 most frequently used words. Visibly, national security is a priority topic, with words "police" and "security" among the top five. The word "environment" is the first climate-related word to appear in this figure and is the 50th most frequent.

Figure 2. Word cloud from tweets.

However, as absolute frequencies are influenced by the level of activity of Twitter profiles, we employed a more in-depth measure of topic prevalence. Text from tweets was aggregated by month, with topic frequencies normalized on a scale from 0 to 1, so that their prevalence is assessed from a comparative perspective.

Figure 3 displays a timeline for the average prevalence of climate, conflict and migration-related topics. Figure 4 presents timelines for the prevalence of climate, conflict, and migration variables in the corpus of tweets. These visualisations reveal not only which topics were in focus, but also when they were of most interest.

Figure 3. Timeline of Tweets that contain climate, conflict and migration-related topics, by month.

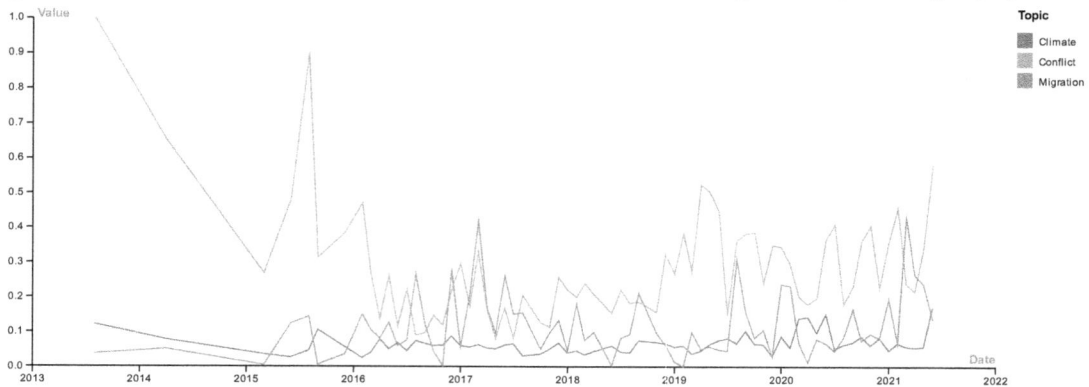

Across the years, there are visible peaks in conflict and migration-related tweets. In some instances, they roughly coincide, and in others, conflict peaks are followed by migration peaks. This is not surprising, as the main reasons for migration and displacement in Nigeria can be linked to the escalated violent activities of Boko Haram since 2014. Further, the period between 2016 and 2019 witnessed an alarming increase in fatalities due to farmer-herder violence, a phenomenon that cannot be completely understood without considering climate-related changes in pastoral migration (ICG 2017, ICG 2018). Compounded by COVID-related impacts, prevalence of conflict and disaster-induced displacements were also reported since 2020 (IDMC 2021, Rigaud et al., 2021). In comparison, climate-related peaks are less prominent, indicating that climate policy and action are underrepresented in social media conversations of state actors.

Among the climate variables, 'Rain' was the most prevalent topic throughout the period of analysis, with major peaks in between 2013-2015. While its prevalence remained relatively stable from 2015 onwards, 2021 shows a steep upward trend in attention to rainfall variability. 'Sea level rise' and 'Drought' have also garnered more attention since 2020.

The conflict timeline shows two substantial peaks for 'Crime', 'Theft' and "Sexual violence" in 2013 and 2015. These three variables often trend together, reflecting a context of violence that involves multiple actors. Regarding migration, a peak prevalence is visible in the first half of 2017, which could be attributed to the launch of the new Immigration Regulations 2017 by Nigeria's Ministry of Interior, and in 2021, which could relate to the development of the National Diaspora Policy.

To understand associations between different topics within tweets, a measure of correlation determines how often they appear together in a tweet, relative to how often they appear separately. Figure 5 displays the seven variables most positively correlated to migration. The strongest pathway that links migration to climate stressors, socioeconomic risks, and conflict is related to agriculture and pastoralism, as narratives about migration were substantially associated to resource management, livestock, yields and productivity, along with refugees, health, and employment. No significant associations between migration and climate or conflict variables were identified. Such gaps in the discourse point to a need for contextual evidence-based action and sensitization around climate security pathways with a focus on migration.

Figure 4. Timeline of tweets about climate (top), conflict (middle) and migration (bottom).

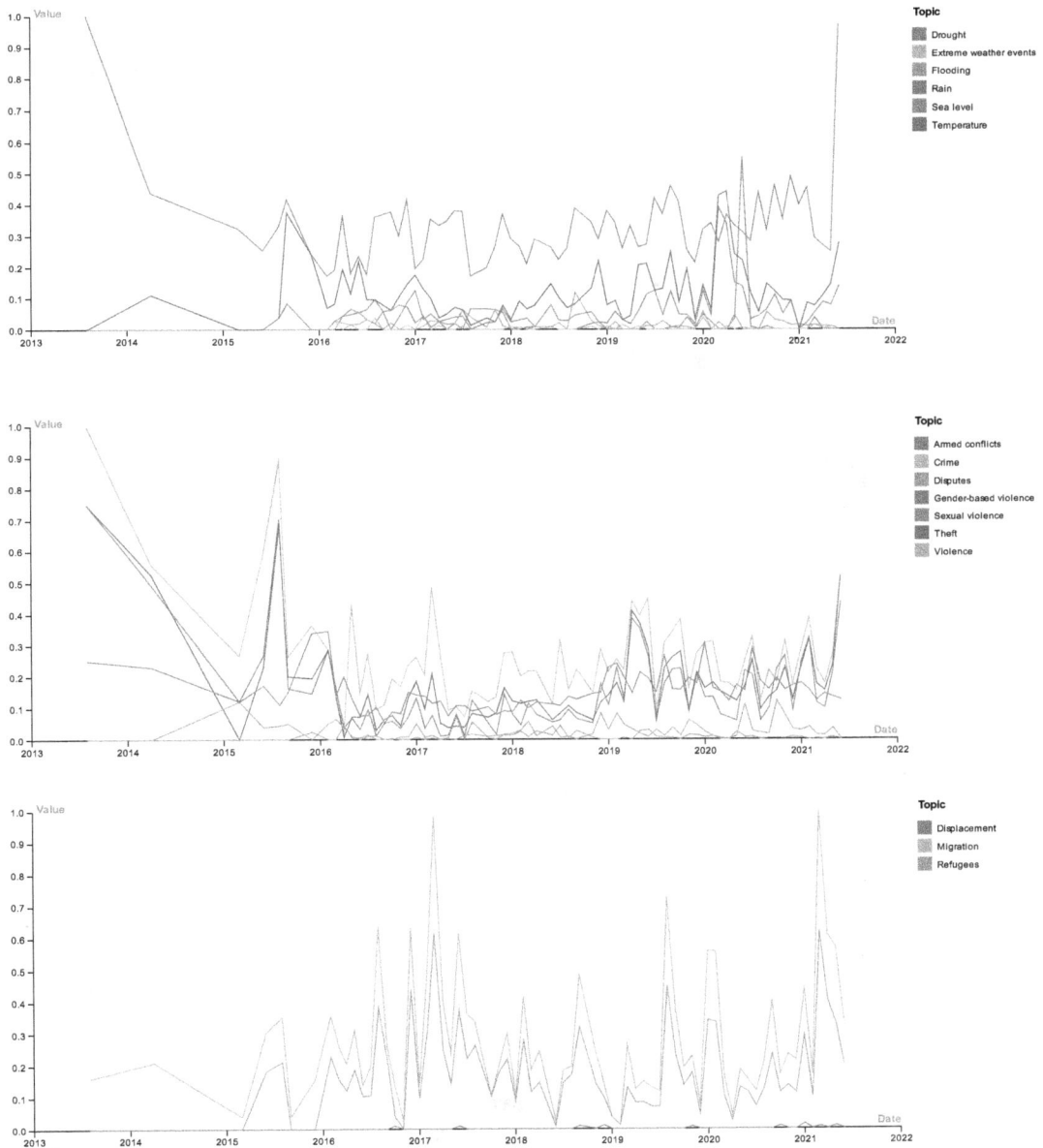

Figure 5. Top 7 correlations between migration and other topics identified the Tweets extracted from the official accounts of selected government bodies.

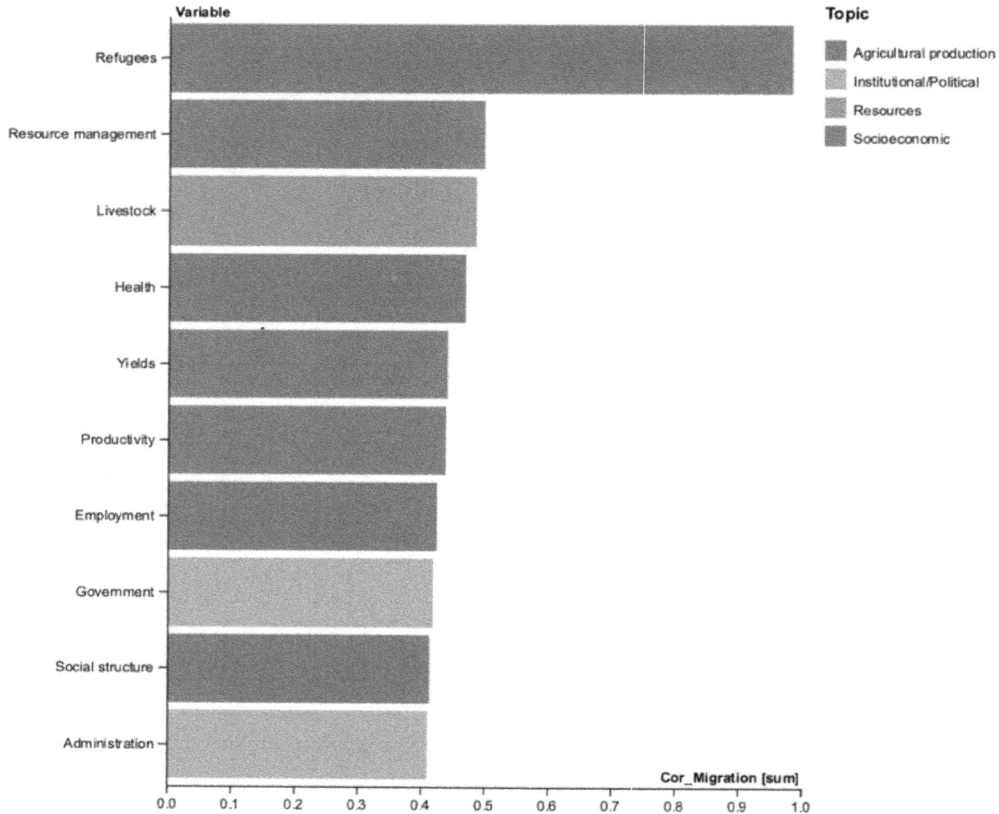

Conclusion

Content analysis techniques enable identification of trends in political agendas and actors over time and across geographies. The digital methods approach employed to explore representations of the climate security-migration nexus in the Twitter communications of Nigerian policy actors found that the pathways that link climate stressors, conflict and migration are not well represented in the social media narratives of government bodies. The absence of strong associations between migration and climate or conflict-related variables indicate a disconnect between climate, security, and migration policy domains.

A limitation of this approach is that social media narratives may not fully capture the complexity of policy cycles in a country like Nigeria, where policy actors interact across multiple scales, their presence and voice not adequately represented in digital spaces. Nevertheless, as the COVID-19 pandemic highlighted, there is an emergent trend to integrate digital platforms in policy and governance during times of crisis. Leveraging this understanding, this study contributes a step towards mapping policymaker perspectives in public discourse, along with identifying gaps and scope in integrating dimensions of the climate security-migration nexus within Nigeria's formal policy arena.

References

Abel, G. J., Brottrager, M., Cuaresma, J. C., & Muttarak, R. (2019). Climate, conflict and forced migration. *Global environmental change, 54*, 239-249.

Barberá P., & Zeitzoff, T. (2018). The New Public Address System: Why Do World Leaders Adopt Social Media? *International Studies Quarterly, 62*, 121–130.

Bertot J. C., Jaeger, P. T., & Hansen, D. (2012). The impact of policies on government social media usage: Issues, challenges, and recommendations, *Government Information Quarterly, 29*(1), 30-40.

Boas, I. et al. (2019). Climate migration myths. *Nature Climate Change, 9*(12), 901-903.

Brzoska, M. (2012). *Climate Change as a Driver of Security Policy BT - Climate Change, Human Security and Violent Conflict: Challenges for Societal Stability.* In J. Scheffran, M. Brzoska, H. G. Brauch, P. M. Link, & J. Schilling (Eds.); pp. 165–184. Springer Berlin Heidelberg.

Brzoska, M., & Fröhlich, C. (2016). Climate change, migration and violent conflict: vulnerabilities, pathways and adaptation strategies. *Migration and Development, 5*(2), 190-210.

Carneiro, B. et al. (2022). What is the importance of climate research? An innovative web-based approach to assess the influence and reach of climate research programs, *Environmental Science & Policy, 133*.

Carneiro, B., Resce, G., & Sapkota, T.B. (2022), Digital artifacts reveal development and diffusion of climate research, *Scientific Reports, 12*, 14146.

Dorff C, Gallop M, Minhas, S. (2020). Networks of violence: Predicting conflict in Nigeria. *The Journal of Politics 82*(2): 476-493.

Dutta Gupta, T. et al. (2021). How does climate exacerbate root causes of conflict in Nigeria? An impact pathway analysis. *CGIAR FOCUS Climate Security Fact Sheet*, https://hdl.handle.net/10568/116271

ICG (International Crisis Group) (2017). Herders against Farmers: Nigeria's Expanding Deadly Conflict. ICG, 19 September 2017, https://www.crisisgroup.org/africa/west-africa/nigeria/252-herders-against-farmers-nigerias-expanding-deadly-conflict

ICG (International Crisis Group). (2018). Stopping Nigeria's Spiralling Farmer-Herder Violence. ICG, 26 July 2018, https://www.crisisgroup.org/africa/west-africa/nigeria/262-stopping-nigerias-spiralling-farmer-herder-violence

IDMC (Internal Displacement Monitoring Centre). (2021). Global Report on Internal Displacement. IDMC. https://www.internal-displacement.org/global-report/grid2021/

IOM (2018*). GCM Global Compact for Safe, Orderly and Regular Migration*, United Nations, New York.

IPCC (2022). Summary for Policymakers [H.-O. Pörtner, D.C. et al. (eds.)]. In: Climate Change 2022: Impacts, Adaptation, and Vulnerability. Contribution of Working Group II to the Sixth Assessment Report of the Intergovernmental Panel on Climate Change Cambridge University Press. In Press.

McDonald, M. (2013). Discourses of climate security. *Political Geography, 33*, 42–51.

Rigaud, K. K. et al. (2021). Groundswell Africa: A Deep Dive into Internal Climate Migration in Nigeria. World Bank, Washington, DC.

Rogers, R. (2013). *Digital methods.* MIT press

Rogers, R., Sanchez-Querubin N., & Kil A. (2015). *Issue Mapping for an Aging Europe*, Amsterdam: Amsterdam University Press.

von Uexkull, N., & Buhaug, H. (2021). Security implications of climate change: A decade of scientific progress. *Journal of Peace Research, 58*(1), 3–17.

World Bank (2021). Nigeria - Overview. https://www. worldbank.org/en/country/nigeria/overview#1

A COLLECTIVE DEEP MAP REPRESENTATION TOOL TO PRODUCE KNOWLEDGE ON INTELLECTUAL EXILE

Maissam Nimer[1]

Who are Qualified Migrants in Exile?

This paper aims to produce knowledge about so-called qualified migrations through a collective project entitled Géo-récits situated at the intersection of several disciplines, namely anthropology, sociology, political science, history and geography. The qualification of highly qualified migrants is contextual and socially constructed and thus not straightforward to define. In this paper, it is defined as individuals with diverse forms of cultural capital: institutionalized culture capital (diplomas, employment…) or incorporated (knowledge of political and social context, through activism, militantism or art) (Bourdieu, 1979 and Matonti and Poupeau, 2004). This definition thus includes militant resources, and learnings imported from other environments or progressively acquired through engagement or experiences in militantism in the political field. Studies in the field of sociology of migration usually insist on the brain drain aspect, and qualified migrants in exile are usually rarely studied, as their skills are often considered as not much adapted to the labour market, or disqualified. The particular characteristics of forced exile on their trajectories after exile are not explored.

The project produces knowledge on qualified migration by representing migration trajectories and narratives of exiled intellectuals and artists through deep maps. It aims to make these (maps) accessible on a user-friendly interface in order to disseminate the products of scientific research to society. They can be in the form of illustrated geographical trajectories that interweave with other biographical representations, memories, interview quotations as well as images, videos and sounds which are displayed chronologically. Deep maps are representations that go beyond the two-dimensional traditional map.

A collaborative Deep Map Research Tool

This project elaborates an extensive collaborative tool, using these deep maps as a starting point, with the goal of collecting data by different research groups and individual researchers working on different geographical areas (Middle East, North Africa, East Europe, Balkan countries, Latin America) and historical periods through different methodologies (in-depth interviews, archive). The goal is to represent movement through these maps to be able to explore trajectories, identifications and strategies of inclusion into the labour market. The collective deep map representation tool allows us to showcase these trajectories and filter them according to predetermined research variables such as gender, languages, passage points, pathways, year of exile, country of origin, among others. Research groups have experimented with deep maps (Baussant, 2018), whereby life stories are decompartmentalized from the territorial anchoring of the migratory studies and the temporalities in which witnesses and researchers are inscribed (Galloro, Pascutto et Serré 2010). The Géo-Récits project goes further by

[1] Assistant Professor, Istanbul University, msnimer@gmail.com, this project is funded by the Institut Convergences Migrations (ICM) and is led by Pascale Laborier.

introducing a collaborative dimension to the deep map representations.

With the help of this tool, we can explore the data of several projects collectively to bring light to new emerging research questions relating to knowledge production in exile across different geographical and historical frames. The purpose is also to raise awareness within the general public on the questions of migration and particularly qualified migration. This is a novel datasource as deep maps allow the representation of stories, materials and their evolution through time while crossing it with the geographical movement. We approach life stories as databases to be analysed for a better understanding of places, their intimate and personal geographies, as well as the structure of the stories that refer to it.

This collective deep map tool represents a different way of capturing migration for broader analysis. It also creates a sample for an open-source database to be used by all researchers who are interested in highly qualified migration, it also serves as a model which can be eventually replicated and adapted to other population and different research questions. This paper presents the deep mapping tool, which is currently under development, to engages about this innovative way of representing migration through data visualisation with the goal of engaging in a collaborative research project and answering different research questions.

Ethical and Methodological Considerations

As part of this presentation, I engage in a reflection on the ethical and methodological considerations in terms of collection and representation of data about migration, namely looking at the difficulties faced in terms of linking individual and collective trajectories in representations. Indeed, the data collection through interviews can expose individuals to relive the trauma related to their forced migration experience, and representing these trajectories can put individuals at risk. As such, I reflect on the possibility of involving interviewees (highly qualified forced migrants) to actively take part in the research process through the co-creation of these deep maps to allow individuals to auto-narrate and represent their own trajectories especially taking into consideration possible reluctance among this population to being considered as 'research objects'.

The concern of putting the refugees in danger, a risk that is increased by visibilisation through our project, can be partly resolved through anonymization or the choice of a pseudonym. However, beyond hiding the name of the person, anonymization implies erasing all data related to personal characteristics which allow the direct or indirect identification of a physical person. Beyond a simple study of prosopographies, this process is not limited to following the traces of migrants and representing them on a map, but rather also revealing their emotions, such as fears and joys, perceived during their trajectories in different cities, countries or at different borders. At the end of their exile journey - an end that is often temporary - the undetermined wait for a legal status in their host country, an improvement of the political situation in their country of origin, not only elongates time, but also thickens the space. Life stories give access to intimate and personal geographies of migrants, without compromising their identity. As such, some of these trajectories cannot be published, as they would be impossible to anonymize without deleting all significant information. In many cases, the situation is rather blurred, whereby the risk of putting the refugee in danger does not seem too significant, yet there is always an unknown factor.

Non-linearity in Space and Time

The project takes into account the diachrony of trajectories, through the superposition of spaces and multiple moments of exile. It associates the map to an interactive chronological strip that allows researchers to visualise different periods in the lives of persons, or institutions. Researchers are faced with the difficulty of localising on the map territories (such as cities or empires) that no longer exist within their actual borders, such as East-Berlin or the Soviet Ukraine. I thus reflect on developing an instrument of diachronic geographical localization that would allow us to add semiological layers, or superpose historical surfaces to the contemporary surface. Diachrony also implies considering the lived space, beyond an itinerary that would be a series of movements. Indeed, if the deep map that we wish to construct is to allow us to shed light on the dynamic of movements, we intend to put forth sedentary moments, places where migrants "stayed".

The question of temporality complexifies even further when we take into account the fact that the experience of exile can create confusion between temporal and spatial entities that become fixed. In other words, the departure place is sometimes essentialized as past, as something that is left behind or that exists in memories only, whereas the host country represents the future, all the more so that it is often the place in which children of exiles are born and raised. At other times, the country of origin is essentialized as a future, a space to which we wish to go back to. As time flows, the space also becomes vaguer: exiles no longer remember street names or exact addresses of places, which implies differentiating different levels of precision of a place. Researchers are thus confronted with the challenge of creating maps that account for the complexity and multiplicity of the spatio-temporal dimensions inherent to each life story. By representing the time associated with each location, we must reflect on whether this location represents the country as it was left, the country as it is remembered or the country as it is now. I also think of different types of links that can exist between locations. Whether departure, arrival, birth, passage, marriage, divorce, naturalisation, work, life and death, all of these places do not have the same importance. They can thus be represented with different colours or intensities. The determination of the level of importance of a location is left to the interpretation - thus the subjectivity - of the researcher, but this is inevitable as the map itself cannot but be subjective («

there is not such a thing as an innocent map", Zwer & Rekacewicz, 2021). Indeed, even if a historical image embodies a historical way of seeing, our seeing of it depends upon "our own way of seeing." (Berger, 2008).

This approach also contributes by allowing us to think beyond the linearity of migration studies from one point to another, to seeing it as a multi-linear process, which is often missed in migration studies. In detailing the multiple steps that constitute the trajectory of a qualified migrant, the Géo-récits project puts forward South-South mobilities (from Uruguay to Argentina, from Syria to Turkey) or North-South migration, especially with regards to return migration, which are more common than expected. This represents an opportunity to shift our glance away from focusing on solely South-North mobilities. This project thus offers a fertile ground for interdisciplinary research, to think differently of contemporary mobilities and their dynamism, as well as the social links and intersubjectivity between North and South.

References

Baussant Michèle, "Un nom éternel qui jamais ne sera effacé", *Terrain*, 65, 2015, 52-75.

Berger John, Ways of Seeing, Penguin Classics, pp. 176, 2008

Bourdieu Pierre, "Les trois états du capital culturel", *Actes de la recherche en sciences sociales*, n°30, 1979, p. 3-6.

Caquard Sébastien and Dimitrovas Stefanie, "Story Maps & Co. Un état de l'art de la cartographie des récits sur Internet", *Mappemonde*, 121, 2017,

Galloro P.-D., Pascutto T. et Serré A. De l'immigré à l'émigré? *Temporalités* 2010, 11. DOI: 10.4000/temporalites.1168

Matonti Frédérique et Poupeau Franck. "Le capital militant. Essai de définition". *Actes de la recherche en sciences sociales*, n° 5/5, 2004, p. 4-11.

Mekdjian Sara, Amilhat-Szary A.-L., Moreau M. et al. (2014). "Figurer les entre-deux migratoires. Pratiques cartographiques expérimentales entre chercheurs, artistes et voyageurs". Carnets de géographes, n° 7, « Les espaces de l'entre-deux », ed. Julie Le Gall and Lionel Rouge.

Rossetto P. (2014). "Juifs de Libye: notes pour une "cartographie" des lieux migratoires". *Archivio Antropologico Mediterraneo*, vol. 16, n° 1, p. 87-99.

Zwer Nephtys, Rekacewicz Philippe, *Cartographie radicale: Explorations*, Paris, La Découverte, 2021

ONE SWALLOW DOES NOT A SUMMER MAKE: POLITICS AND THE INTERPRETATION OF ABS MIGRATION DATA IN SOUTH AUSTRALIA DURING THE COVID-19 PANDEMIC

Garry Goddard[1], Adam Graycar[2], Romy Wasserman[3], and George Tan[4]

Introduction

In Australia interstate migration is highly competitive and politically contentious, and thus measurement is important. This paper examines the political use of official – Australian Bureau of Statistics (ABS) – migration statistics in the State of South Australia (SA) during the COVID-19 pandemic, where a (small) reversal in long-term interstate migration trends has occurred.

The former Premier, Steven Marshall, aimed to lift SA's population growth rate to the national average. His policy platform came together in the "Magnet State" program, which included marketing campaigns and a range of other activities aimed at attracting and retaining young entrepreneurs and talented under 40s from other parts of Australia.

ABS data shows that SA had a positive net interstate migration of 704 people for the 2020-21 financial year. This is one of only three occasions since the mid-1980s when SA has recorded more interstate arrivals than departures (the others being 1984 and 1991).

Despite these very small numbers, Steven Marshall touted the ABS statistics as a sign that his policies were working and the state had turned the demographic corner. A cynic may simply see border closures and travel restrictions in response to COVID-19 as temporarily halting the usual outflow of young talent to greener pastures. The most recent ABS data release suggests the cynics may well be right.

Background

South Australia's population stands at 1.7 million, the smallest of the mainland Australian states, accounting for just over 7 percent of the total Australian population. Though its population continues to grow, the rate of growth is low compared to eastern states and the national average. As Figure 1 shows, SA's population change generally reflects variations at a national level but at growth rates below one percent for most of the past two decades. At the same time, SA has long grappled with the challenging trifecta of an ageing population, declining fertility and net interstate migration losses.

[1] Visiting Research Fellow, Stretton Institute of Public Policy, University of Adelaide, Australia. E-mail: garrygoddard@bigpond.com
[2] Professor of Public Policy and Director of the Stretton Institute of Public Policy, University of Adelaide, Australia.
E-mail: adam.graycar@adelaide.edu.au
[3] Research Associate, Hugo Centre for Migration and Population Studies, University of Adelaide, Australia.
E-mail: romy.wasserman@adelaide.edu.au
[4] Lecturer, Department of Geography, Environment and Population, University of Adelaide and Adjunct Fellow, Northern Institute, Charles Darwin University. E-mail: george.tan@adelaide.edu.au

Figure 1. Australia and South Australia: rate of population growth per annum, 1947 - 2021

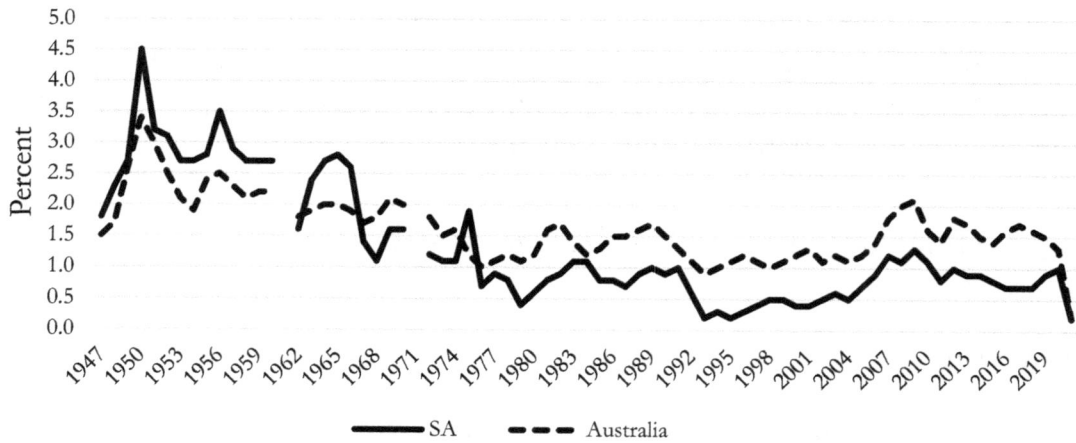

Source: ABS Australian Historical Population Statistics, 2019; ABS National, State and Territory Population (various releases). Note: Gaps in data indicate changes in methodology.

In this context, overseas migration is an important driver of population growth. In fact, it has been the backbone of growth since the mid-2000s (Figure 2). Immigration has also changed the composition of SA's population, with a quarter of the population born overseas in more than 200 different birthplaces, and speaking approximately 180 languages (ABS, 2016).

Figure 2. South Australia: components of population change 1990 - 2021

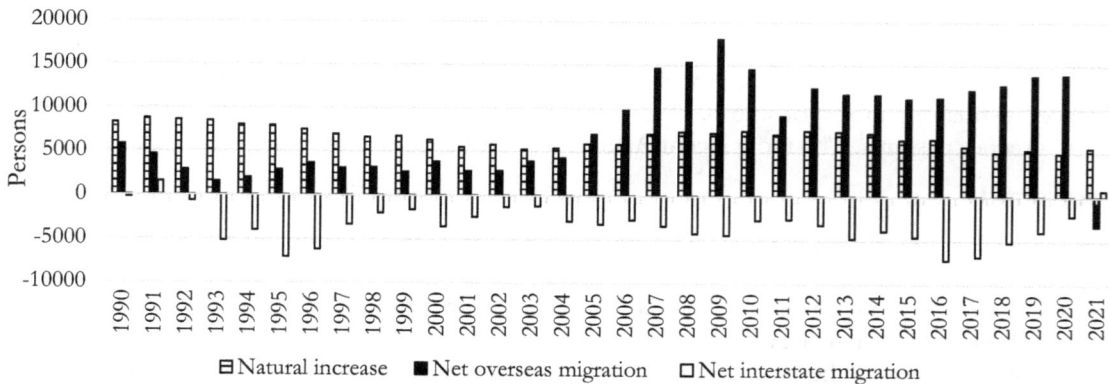

Source: ABS Australian Demographic Statistics (various releases); ABS National, State and Territory Population (various releases).

But an equally important element of population dynamics is interstate migration, specifically the entrenched losses of people interstate (see Figure 2). As far back as the state's economic woes of the 1990s, flows out of SA have typically been selective of young, well-educated people, posing serious economic and demographic consequences (Hugo, 2002). Since 2010, three quarters of those leaving have moved to Victoria (31.9 %), Queensland (22.9%) and NSW (21.8 %) (ABS stat data, 2021).

Policy Response – the Marshall Plan

Successive SA governments have attempted to drive economic growth and diversify the state's economy through a range of investment attraction policies and technology precincts over the past thirty odd years. Some have prioritised population policy and some have not.

The Rann Labor Government (2002-2011) developed a *State Strategic Plan* to set targets for all areas of public policy, including a population target to "increase South Australia's population to 2 million by 2050 with an interim target of 1.64 million by 2014." (GSA, 2007, Target T 1.22) The subsequent Weatherill Labor Government (2011-2018) retained the State Strategic Plan, but was less focused on population policy *per se* and gravitated toward more typical state development strategies.

Most recently, the Marshall Liberal Government (2018-2022) tweaked this approach to focus on growth areas like space technology, start-ups and cyber-security, but they also linked this to an explicit population strategy to support those sectors and drive economic growth more broadly – *Magnet State*.

Whilst not adopted as a hard target, Steven Marshall talked in aspirational terms about lifting the state's population growth rate to the national average – i.e. from circa 0.7-0.8% to circa 1.6%. per annum – or, in terms of migration arrivals, " … we want to get closer to the national population growth rate, which means we would need more than 20,000 people per year, and what we inherited … was around 10,000 people per year" (Penberthy, 2019).

However, this population strategy also had a focus on creative industries, start-ups and the entrepreneurial ecosystem in targeting young entrepreneurs and talented under 40s from other parts of Australia (Washington, 2020). This approach underpins the broader Magnet State program, which draws heavily on research undertaken previously by KPMG regarding the attractiveness of certain cities to young wealth-creators around the globe and how cities facing economic and population decline can turn this around (KPMG, 2014).

Funding for Magnet State was provided in December 2021, with $12.3 million allocated over three financial years to fund a "population growth strategy", of which the core components were:

- Increased awareness of South Australia in the eastern states through a marketing campaign in key demographics

- An online jobs platform to provide information on career opportunities in South Australia

- Industry engagement to identify current and future workforce needs

- A graduate scheme to connect employers in Growth State sectors with a pool of graduates (GSA, 2021, pp. 42-43).

COVID-19 Shocks and Political Interpretations

Globally, the outbreak of COVID-19 effectively stopped the movement of people across and within borders. In Australia, international borders were closed in late March 2020 only to be opened again nearly two years later in February 2022. Limited flights carrying Australian citizens, permanent residents and a small number of exempted travelers were permitted to enter, but ultimately there was a massive decline in net overseas migration nationally.

In SA, too, net overseas migration plummeted and along with it population growth, which fell to 0.2 % in the year ending June 2021 (Figure 3). But the pandemic also disrupted the usual patterns of internal migration, with extended lockdowns and strict state and territory border closures severely reducing mobility. As Figure 3 shows, the only-just-alive rate of population growth in SA for 2020-21 was supported by a small and surprising reversal of net interstate migration into positive territory. The last time this happened was in 1991.

Figure 3. South Australia: net overseas and net interstate migration with population growth (%)

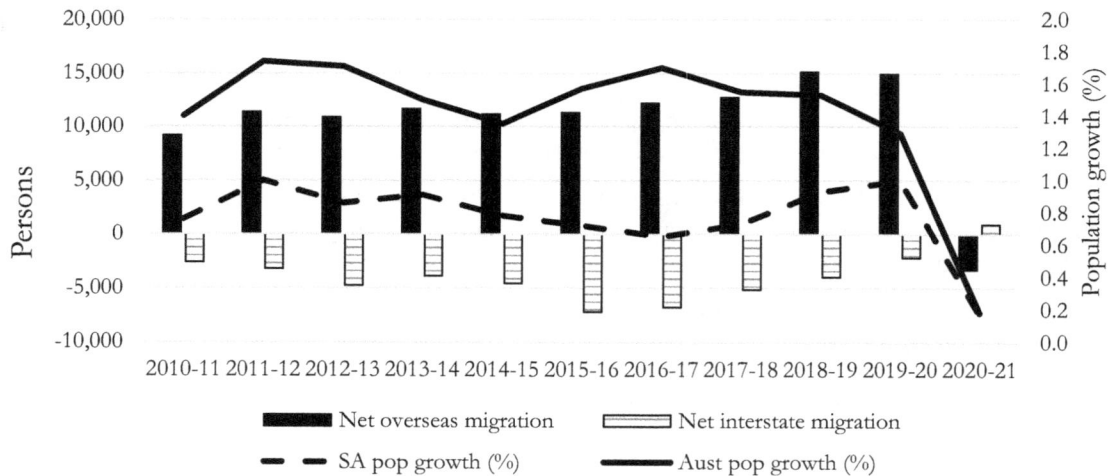

Source: ABS Australian Demographic Statistics (various releases); ABS Overseas Migration 2020-21; ABS National, State and Territory Population (various releases).

Quarterly figures show net interstate migration gains in SA from June 2020 to March 2021 (Table 1). It is clear these gains are not the result of more people coming from interstate, with arrivals through 2020 and early 2021 on par with, or slightly lower, than the two years prior to the outbreak. Rather, fewer people left SA during the worst of the pandemic with 4,000-6,000 people leaving each quarter

Table 1. South Australia: quarterly interstate arrivals, departures and net interstate migration through COVID-19, March 2018 to September 2021

		Interstate arrivals	Interstate departures	Net interstate migration
	March	6155	7246	-1091
	June	5967	6956	-989
	September	5472	6233	-761
2018	December	7098	8481	-1383
	March	6253	7155	-902
2019	June	6153	7065	-912
	September	5389	6381	-992
	December	6808	7863	-1055
	March	5736	5953	-217
2020	June	5793	5689	104
	September	5015	4872	143
	December	6613	6311	302
	March	6932	6193	739
2021	June	8028	8317	-289
	September	9877	10068	-191

Source: ABS National, State and Territory Population (various releases).

compared to a quarterly average of around 7,000 in the previous two years. But with the lifting of restrictions later in 2021, including the opening of domestic borders, interstate travel to and from SA increased substantially to reach higher than pre-COVID levels in June and September 2021 when, once again, departures surpassed arrivals.

After ABS data was released showing SA had its third straight quarter of net population gain, the then Premier put out a press release claiming the data as evidence of not only a strong economic recovery from the COVID-19 pandemic, but also as a sign that the state had reversed a long-standing demographic trend:

> While the former Labor government presided over a dreadful brain drain interstate, we are turning the tide and transforming the state through our safe and strong handling of the COVID pandemic.
>
> Business confidence is also high, we are smashing new home building approvals, single touch payroll figures show employment is strong, and net interstate migration is the best it's been for almost thirty years (Craig, 2021).

As table 1 shows, the overall net gain for the quarter was 302 people, compared to a loss of 1,055 for the same quarter a year earlier and an annual average loss in the order of 5,000-6,000 people over the previous decade.

Conclusion

As border closures and travel restrictions unwind, it will become much clearer the extent to which the state has turned the demographic corner or simply returned to the long-term demographic trend.

The most recent ABS figures (for the September Quarter 2021) show the state had a net loss of 191 people to interstate migration and net loss of 1,385 people to net overseas migration, with the total net migration figure for SA being the worst ever recorded (Spence, 2022).

It appears as though we are simply returning to the long-term trend.

There is always a temptation for politicians to attribute real world outcomes to their policy initiatives, but it is rarely that clear cut. With the full policy package announced only in December 2021, it is simply not possible for Magnet State *per se* to have impacted either the quarterly or annual ABS results. The real causal factors were kicking-in almost 18 months earlier, the timing of which is more closely aligned to the imposition of COVID-19 travel restrictions and border closures stopping people leaving the state (Richardson, 2022).

Interestingly, having lost the 19th of March 2022 State Election, Steven Marshall chose to single out stopping the "brain drain" as one of his Government's most significant achievements in his Concession Speech. An unusual accolade for population policy. It appears, however, that this achievement is most likely a short-term statistical anomaly driven by the public health responses to the COVID-19 pandemic.

References

Australian Bureau of Statistics (ABS). (2016). *Australian Bureau of Statistics Census of Population and Housing, TableBuilder data* [Dataset] https://www.abs.gov.au/statistics/microdata-tablebuilder/tablebuilder

Australian Bureau of Statistics (ABS). (2019). *Australian Historical Population Statistics 2019*, Catalogue number 3105.0.65.001. ABS. [Dataset] https://www.abs.gov.au/statistics/people/population/historical-population/2016#data-download

Australian Bureau of Statistics (ABS). (2021). *Australian Demographic Statistics* (various releases). ABS. [Dataset] https://www.abs.gov.au/statistics/people/population/national-state-and-territory-population

Australian Bureau of Statistics (ABS). (2021). *National, State and Territory Population* (various releases). ABS. [Dataset] https://www.abs.gov.au/statistics/people/population/national-state-and-territory-population/latest-release

Australian Bureau of Statistics (ABS). (2021). *Overseas Migration 2020-21*. ABS. [Dataset] https://www.abs.gov.au/statistics/

people/population/overseas-migration/2020-21

ABS stat data. (2021). *Interstate Migration by States and Territories of Arrival and Departure by Sex*. ABS. [Dataset] https://explore.data.abs.gov.au/vis?tm=quarterly%20population&pg=0&df[ds]=ABS_ABS_TOPICS&df[id]=ABS_D EM_QIM&df[ag]=ABS&df[vs]=1.0.0&hc[Frequency]=Quarterly&pd=2010-Q1%2C2021-Q3&dq=3.4..Q&ly[rw]=STATE_ARR&ly[cl]=TIME_PERIOD&vw=tb`

Craig, L. (2021, May 9). Adelaide sees biggest migration surge in three decades. *Glam Adelaide*. https://glamadelaide.com.au/adelaide-sees-biggest-migration-surge-in-three-decades/

Government of South Australia (GSA). (2007, January). *South Australia's Strategic Plan*. Updated Version. GSA. Adelaide.

Government of South Australia (GSA). (2021, December). *Mid-Year Budget Review 2021-22*. GSA. Adelaide. https://www.treasury.sa.gov.au/budget/current-budget/2021-22/Mid-Year-Budget-Review-2021-22.pdf

Hugo, G. (2002). A population policy for South Australia? *People and Place*, 10(3), 1-10.

KPMG. (2014, July). *Magnet Cities: decline | fightback | victory*. KPMG. UK. www.kpmg.com/uk/magnetcities

Penberthy, D. (2019, September 14). South Australia seeks formula to reverse exodus. *The Australian*. https://www.theaustralian.com.au/inquirer/south-australia-seeks-formula-to-reverse-exodus/news-story/242c00bf6e0ab3a61df97f7903fed8af

Richardson, T. (2022, February 28). Marshall chose to under promise – but is there time to deliver? *In Daily*. https://indaily.com.au/opinion/2022/02/28/richardson-marshall-chose-to-underpromise-but-is-there-time-to-deliver/

Spence, A. (2022, March 23). SA population shrinks as 'brain drain' resumes. *In Daily*. https://indaily.com.au/news/2022/03/23/sa-population-shrinks-as-brain-drain-resumes/

Washington, D. (2020, July 15). Marshall's plan to make Adelaide a "magnet" for under-40s. *In Daily*. https://indaily.com.au/news/2020/07/15/marshalls-plan-to-make-adelaide-a-magnet-for-under-40s/

RESTRICTION OF THE RIGHT TO FREEDOM OF MOVEMENT: MIGRATION, PANDEMIC, AND THE AEGEAN BORDER REGIME

Panagiotis Mavroudis[1]

The COVID-19 pandemic shook medical and healthcare standards in the global north, and re-contextualised considerations about human rights tenets in the *syndemic* of social inequality (Horton, 2020). For racialised poor who already faced the "continental quarantining" of European borders (Achiume, 2019, as cited in Meer, 2022, p. 102) the coronavirus emergency compounded existing challenges of multiple bordering and xenophobic discourse (OHCHR, 2020). This paper aims to trace continuities, intersections, and new challenges of addressing exclusion for racialised migrants by taking the mobility regulation in the recent reception-asylum and pandemic-related legislation in the Greek Aegean border islands as a case study.

The freedom of movement of migrants arriving by sea to Greek border islands was first restricted in March 2016, through the implementation of the *EU- Turkey Statement* (Statement) of the same year and the EU's *hotspot approach* (European Commission, 2015). The Statement considered Turkey a *safe third country* (as defined by Art. 38 of the Directive 2013/32/EU) to undertake the protection of Syrian refugees, as well as the readmission of rejected asylum applicants. The hotspot approach, designed for the "concentrated cooperation" of international, EU and local agencies in camp-like reception facilities, aimed at registration of migrants, rapid asylum procedures and return operations. The Aegean border was "institutionalised" and rendered into a regime of "conflict and negotiation" (Vradis et al., 2019, p. 8; Hess, 2012), the local asylum procedure being the only accessible legal channel to European territory.

The geographical restriction of all asylum applicants entering the islands from Turkey (Director of the Asylum Service, 2017) realised relevant provisions of Directive 2013/33/EU; however, the initial act imposing the immobilisation of migrants was annulled by the supreme national administrative court (*Greek Council for Refugees v. Ministry of Migration Policy*, 2018), which rejected the necessity of the restriction and highlighted its disproportionate impact on local communities. Although the Court did not directly assess the migrants' harmed rights as such, the judgement reflected and indirectly linked the migrants' degraded living conditions in the congested infrastructure and their agency with the affected lives of local communities, balancing them against the objectives of the migration policy of the period. In the following years, the European Court of Human Rights communicated several cases against Greece considering claims of inhuman and degrading treatment in the islands' facilities (*A.R. and others v. Greece*, 2021). However, the act was effectively reintroduced by integrating the judgement's remarks and has remained in force to date. In this framework, the interrelation and conflict of legal variables such as the quality and speed of asylum procedures, the living conditions and the "population management", have raised persisting challenges for the foundations of the proportional equality principle, in terms of framing both the right to freedom of movement and international protection (see

[1] MPhil/PhD Law, Birkbeck College, London, UK. E-mail: panosmavroudis@protonmail.com.
Acknowledgement: Funded by the AHRC CHASE Doctoral Training Partnership.

more in FRA, 2019). Moreover, the new law *on international protection* (2019), which was introduced shortly before the pandemic's outbreak, relativised and incorporated the *vulnerability* concept in the hotspots management framework, entrusting the facilities' directors with extended discretion to individually lift the geographical restriction of movement for certain categories of asylum applicants.

March 2020 was a turning point. The outbreak of the pandemic in the country and the first preventative measures were introduced in a context in which both migrants crossing the Greek-Turkish land borders and the new coronavirus were described by the government's spokesman as "asymmetric threats" causing a "double crisis" (ANA-MPA, 2020) and the first reports of violent "pushbacks" at sea came to light (Keady-Tabbal and Mann, 2020). The government suspended access to asylum and imposed a "seamless web of restrictions" for over two and a half months (Tsourdi and Vavoula, 2021). Restriction of movement and healthcare provisions, codified as the *Agnodiki* plan, were imposed on thousands of migrants remaining on the islands after the pandemic's outbreak. The plan was not officially published, but rather revealed through press leaks, and set the mixed goals of managing "cases of riots, violence, public health risks and big natural disasters" in the congested facilities (Heinrich Böll Stiftung, 2020). According to the plan, specialised measures would be needed for the protection "of the population, as well as the rest of the [country's] population" (NCHR, 2020). Agnodiki did not follow the spirit of the international guidelines for the pandemic for "camp and camp-like settings" by, for instance, allowing positively diagnosed cases to move outside of the congested camps (see more in IASC, 2020). Instead, whenever coronavirus infections appeared in these facilities, the whole area was quarantined, with police blockades guarding the entrance and exit of the "critical perimeter" around the facilities (NCHR, 2020; Inside Story, 2020).

Agnodiki has been accompanied by a binding legal framework regulating migrant accommodation structures to date (See *Annex II* in Joint Ministerial Decision, 2022). Exiting such facilities has been only allowed "for covering basic needs" during the day, according to "police's operational plans". For the general population of Greece, including visiting tourists, pandemic restrictive measures have fluctuated from 2020 to date, according to the experts' recommendations (Art. 1(4) of the Act of Legislative Content of 25.02.2020), remaining at a minimum during tourist seasons (The Guardian, 2020; Reuters, 2021). However, the night curfew and core provisions for areas hosting restricted migrants remained unaltered in the consecutively renewed *Joint Ministerial Decisions* (2022) regulating general pandemic measures, without further assessment and special justification of their necessity and proportionality. On the one hand, reports proved that the risk of infection has been significantly higher in the overwhelmed facilities than for the general population (Kondilis et al., 2021); on the other hand, the population residing in these facilities was allowed to decrease under the existing legal framework for asylum applicants' reception. However, the concerns of the measures applied or omitted in these settings are not only a matter of proportionate lawmaking and balancing of the rights of people who have not been able to reside in their own homes during the pandemic outbreak. Rather, the symbolically explicit contradiction of the Agnodiki's provision regarding the protection of and from the population residing in the camp-like centres marked multiple layers of exceptional restrictions and implicitly disparate objectives, in what was called a "case study of *othering*" (Tsourdi and Vavoula, 2021). The protective discourse of pandemic law restrictions, thus intersected with increased administrative and policing discretion, barriers for legal residence and public space segregation, and further blurred the lines of control and protection for racialized migrants, leading to what Moreno-Lax (2018) has described as a "life-without-full-rights".

The obscurities of the laconic *Annex II* have cast a shadow of uncertainty over the legality of mobility for camp residents and their consequent access to rights and services, leaving space for arbitrary interpretation. While larger camp-like *Closed Controlled Access Centers* were founded on the islands, the "facility resident" turned into an increasingly dominant administrative category to describe migrants of different profiles and legal statuses. For instance, the right of beneficiaries of international protection to autonomously move out of the facilities has been exceptionalised. It is now dependent on the discretion of the administration, according to the provisions of *Annex II*. At the same time, Agnodiki provisions of a police-controlled "perimeter" around the overpopulated old camp-like facilities not only indirectly reflected for the first time the reality of the makeshift favelas in law but assimilated them into the facilities' main infrastructure. Furthermore, the law did not specify if facilities' residents are expected to cumulatively abide by general pandemic-related regulations within their exceptional forms of movement (e. g. visiting a pharmacy). According to published Police statistics, seven times more fines were imposed on non-Greek nationals for pandemic-related offences than on Greek citizens on the islands during the *lockdowns* (AYS, 2021), raising questions of discriminative policing, and highlighting procedural challenges of "measuring" and judicially proving racial profiling. An indicative case, which led to an intervention of the national ombudsperson, was the practice of the port authority of Chios island to impose 5,000 euros fines on asylum applicants for not carrying COVID-19 certificates upon their arrival according to the pandemic-related entry protocol (The Greek Ombudsman, 2022). Last but not least, in 2021 Greece unilaterally defined Turkey as a *safe third country* to undertake most asylum applicants' cases, not only for Syrian but also for Afghani, Somali, Pakistani and Bangladeshi citizens (Joint Ministerial Decision, 2021). This has not only posed a risk of *chain refoulement* in case of their return to Turkey (see more in Fenix, 2022) but has also led them to a prolonged precarity of residence and access to rights in Greece, given the *de facto* suspension of any return operations by Turkey (Bluett, 2021).

Extraordinary rights restrictions and expanded powers have marked the legal landscape of governing the mobility of migrants crossing the Aegean Sea to seek access to Europe. The intersection of reforms in reception and asylum law with the pandemic-related legislation has gradually led to phenomena of legal uncertainty and potentials for socio-spatial segregation of migrants, not only due to existing gaps in legal residence options (Christopoulos, 2020, pp. 82-83) but also under a thick legislative net and arbitrary administration (see First Instance Administrative Court of Syros, 2021). Repeated reports about "increasing violence and human rights violations" in Greece's land and sea borders (UNHCR, 2022), as well as legally unjustified distinctions between "real and non-real" refugees by governmental officials following the war in Ukraine (ERTnews, 2022), have raised concerns of an increasingly racialised reading of international human rights tenets. However, the example of multifaceted restriction or prohibition of movement for asylum-applying migrants in the Aegean has showcased a less immediate questioning of their rights through a gradual transposition of their thresholds. The accumulation of often contradictive or unclear objectives in law, such as population management, asylum procedures, reception guarantees and public health protection, the multilayered legal uncertainty regarding everyday movement and residence, as well as the persisting question of clarity and justification in rights' balancing and specialised needs assessment raises concerns not only regarding a cumulative relativisation of migrants' fundamental rights but also about the challenges of addressing inequalities and "measuring" discrimination in law and legal implementation during but also beyond the pandemic.

References

A.R. and others v. Greece, Application Nos. 59841/19 and 7 other applications (European Court of Human Rights, communicated on 4 January 2021).

Achiume, E. Tendayi. (2019). Migration as Decolonization. *Stanford Law Review 71*, 1509-1574. https://ssrn.com/abstract=3330353

Are You Syrious? (2021, May 28). *AYS Special from Samos: For No Other Reason Than Your Skin Colour.* https://medium.com/are-you-syrious/ays-special-from-samos-for-no-other-reason-than-your-skin-colour-596b15d10920

Athens News Agency-Macedonian Press Agency. (March 26, 2020). *St. Petsas: We Are Successfully Dealing with the Asymmetric Threat of Migration and so We Will Also Deal with the Coronavirus Threat.* https://www.amna.gr/print/443715

Bluett, K. (2021, November 10). *Living in Limbo: The Impact of Greece's Safe Third Country Policy on Afghan Asylum Seekers.* Just Security. https://www.justsecurity.org/79134/living-in-limbo-the-impact-of-greeces-safe-third-country-policy-on-afghan-asylum-seekers/

Chondrogiannos, T. (2020, April 23). Measures and fears considering refugees' protection from coronavirus. *Inside Story.* https://insidestory.gr/article/covid19-metra-fovoi-prostasia-prosfygon-koronois

Christopoulos, D. (2020). If refugees were a problem, there would have been a solution. Polis.

Delanty, G. (Ed.). (2021). Pandemics, politics, and society: Critical perspectives on the covid-19 crisis. De Gruyter.

Designation of third countries that are characterized as safe and compilation of a national list, according to the provisions of article 86 of law 4636/2019 (A 169) 2021 Joint Ministerial Decision 42799/2021, OG 2425/B/07.06.2021 (GR).

Emergency measures for the protection of public health from the risk of further spread of the coronavirus COVID-19 in the country from Monday, May 16, 2022, at 06:00 until Wednesday, June 1, 2022, at 06:00 Joint Ministerial Decision 27397/2020, OG 2369/B/14.05.2022 (GR).

Emergency measures of prevention and limitation of the contagion of the coronavirus 2020 Act of Legislative Content OG 42/A/25.02.2020 (GR).

European Commission. (2015). *Hotspot Approach.* Migration and Home Affairs. https://ec.europa.eu/home-affairs/pages/glossary/hotspot-approach_en

European Union Agency for Fundamental Rights. (2019). *Update of the 2016 FRA Opinion on fundamental rights in the hotspots set up in Greece and Italy.* https://fra.europa.eu/en/publication/2019/update-2016-fra-opinion-fundamental-rights-hotspots-set-greece-and-italy

Fallon, K. (2020, May 27). Greece ready to welcome tourists as refugees stay locked down in Lesbos. *The Guardian.* https://www.theguardian.com/global-development/2020/may/27/greece-ready-to-welcome-tourists-as-refugees-stay-locked-down-in-lesbos-coronavirus

Fenix - Humanitarian Legal Aid. (2022, April 11). Six Years Since Europe's Deal with Turkey. *Border Criminologies. Oxford Law Faculty.* https://www.law.ox.ac.uk/research-subject-groups/centre-criminology/centreborder-criminologies/blog/2022/04/six-years-europes

Grafakou, Danai. (March 16, 2022) *N. Mitarachi on the First Programme: Ukrainian refugees are welcome throughout Europe.* ERTnews. https://www.ertnews.gr/roi-idiseon/n-mitarakis-sto-proto-oi-prosfyges-tis-oykranias-einai-eyprosdektoi-se-oli-tin-eyropi-audio/.

Greek Council for Refugees v. Ministry of Migration Policy 805 Council of State, Chamber D (2018).

Heinrich Böll Stiftung. (2020). *COVID-19 (also) in Moria: Deficient management of the pandemic as utilisation of refugees.* https://gr.boell.org/el/2020/09/22/o-covid-19-kai-sti-moria-i-elleimmatiki-antimetopisi-tis-pandimias-os-ergaleiopoiisi-ton

Hess, S. (2012). De-naturalising transit migration. Theory and methods of an ethnographic regime analysis. *Population, Space and Place, 18*(4), 428–440. https://doi.org/10.1002/psp.632

Horton, R. (2020). Offline: COVID-19 is not a pandemic. *The Lancet, 396*(10255). https://doi.org/10.1016/S0140-6736(20)32000-6

International Federation of Red Cross, International Organization for Migration, United Nations High Commissioner for Refugees & World Health Organization. (2020). *Scaling-up COVID-19 outbreak readiness and response operations in humanitarian situations Including Camps and Camp-Like Settings* (1.1). Inter-Agency Standing Committee. https://interagencystandingcommittee.org/camp-coordination-and-management/interim-guidance-scaling-covid-19-outbreak-readiness-and-response-operations-camps-and-camp-settings

Keady-Tabbal, N., & Mann, I. (2020, May 22). *Tents at Sea: How Greek Officials Use Rescue Equipment for Illegal Deportations.* Just Security. https://www.justsecurity.org/70309/tents-at-sea-how-greek-officials-use-rescue-equipment-for-illegal-deportations/

Kondilis, E., Papamichail, D., McCann, S., Carruthers, E., Veizis, A., Orcutt, M., & Hargreaves, S. (2021). The impact of the COVID-19 pandemic on refugees and asylum seekers in Greece: A retrospective analysis of national surveillance data from 2020. *EClinicalMedicine, 37*(100958). https://doi.org/10.1016/j.eclinm.2021.100958

Kostarakos, M. (2020, April 3). Turkish hybrid operations at our borders: The invasion has already started. *Kathimerini.* https://www.kathimerini.gr/politics/1067577/toyrkikes-yvridikes-epicheiriseis-sta-synora-mas-i-eisvoli-echei-idi-archisei/

Meer, N. (2022). The Cruel Optimism of Racial Justice. Policy Press.

Moreno-Lax, V. (2018). The EU Humanitarian Border and the Securitization of Human Rights: The 'Rescue-Through-Interdiction/Rescue-Without-Protection' Paradigm. *JCMS: Journal of Common Market Studies, 56*(1), 119–140. https://doi.org/10.1111/jcms.12651

National Commission for Human Rights. (2020). *Report on migration and refugees' issues* (B). https://www.nchr.gr/images/

pdf/apofaseis/prosfuges_metanastes/Ekthesi_Anaforas_Prosfugiko_el_compressed.pdf

Objections (on detention) before the Administrative Court of First Instance of Syros AP 36 Administrative Court (2021). https://caselaw.euaa.europa.eu/pages/viewcaselaw.aspx?CaseLawID=2351&returnurl=/pages/digest.aspx

Office of the United Nations High Commissioner for Human Rights. (2020). *Racial discrimination in the context of COVID-19 crisis.* https://www.ohchr.org/sites/default/files/Documents/Issues/Racism/COVID-19_and_Racial_Discrimination.pdf

Regarding International Protection and other provisions 2019 Law 4636/2019, OG 169/A/01.11.2019 (GR).

Restriction movement of applicants for international protection 2017 Director of the Asylum Service 10464/31.5.2017, OG 1977/B/7.6.2017 (GR).

Restriction of movement in facilities hosting asylum seekers 2020 Joint Ministerial Decision 20030/2020, OG 985/B/21.04.2020 (GR).

Reuters. (2021, May 15). *"I'm finally here": Greece formally opens to tourists.* https://www.reuters.com/world/europe/im-finally-here-greece-formally-opens-tourists-2021-05-15/

Tsourdi, E. (Lilian), & Vavoula, N. (2021). Killing me Softly? Scrutinising the Role of Soft Law in Greece's Response to COVID-19. *European Journal of Risk Regulation*, *12*(1), 59–76. https://doi.org/10.1017/err.2020.114

United Nations High Commissioner for Refugees. (February 21, 2022) *News Comment: UNHCR Warns of Increasing Violence and Human Rights Violations at European Borders.* https://www.unhcr.org/news/press/2022/2/62137a284/news-comment-unhcr-warns-increasing-violence-human-rights-violations-european.html

Vradis, A., Papada, E., Painter, J., & Papoutsi, A. (2019). *New borders: Hotspots and the European migration regime.* Pluto Press.

Walters, W. (2012). Foucault and Frontiers: Notes on the Birth of the Humanitarian Border. In U. Bröckling, S. Krasmann, & T. Lemke (Eds.), *Governmentality: Current issues and future challenges* (pp. 138–164). Routledge, Taylor & Francis Group.

THE IMPACT OF THE COVID-19 PANDEMIC ON THE UNITED KINGDOM'S IMMIGRATION DETENTION SYSTEM

Ayesha Riaz[1]

Introduction

Unlike most European countries, the United Kingdom (UK) has not legislated a statutory upper time limit regarding the period an individual can be held in immigration detention (All Party Parliamentary Group on Refugees, 2016). In fact, the UK detains three times more individuals in immigration detention as compared to other European Member States (Association of Visitors of Immigration Detainees, 2019).

The power to detain individuals was created by virtue of paragraphs 16.1-2 of Schedule 2 of the Immigration Act 1971, which is still applicable today. As per this provision there is a presumption against the use of immigration detention and so a person can be detained in conjunction with any of these administrative acts; namely when a claim is being examined, or if a person is pending removal or deportation. Asylum seekers fall into the first category as they may wait many months or even years for a decision on their application for leave to enter (an asylum seeker may be detained on entry in order to decide whether to grant leave to enter or reasons to exist) is granted. The UK immigration 'detention estate' comprises immigration removal centres, short-term holding facilities, pre-departure accommodation and prisons for foreign national offenders (Waterman, Pillay, Katona, 2021).

This chapter will firstly consider how the UK dealt with immigration detention following the outbreak of COVID-19 in 2020. It is clear that the UK's response to the pandemic was poor which prompted detained individuals to lodge a number of legal challenges, some of which have been discussed below. Thus, this pandemic showed us firstly that the detainees/migrants are at the peril of the State, and secondly that the UK can limit the use of administrative detention as detention numbers plummeted during the height of the pandemic. One can measure the benefits of migration from making use of alternatives to detention also, as migrants integrate into the communities they reside in (discussed below). Thus, this chapter will conclude by arguing that the UK should make more widespread use of alternatives to detention and severely limit or abolish administrative detention altogether.

The UK's reaction to COVID-19 vis-à-vis Immigration Detention

Concerns were raised about the appropriateness of immigration detention during the first few months of the COVID-19 outbreak after the first immigration detainee tested positive for COVID-19 around March 2020 (Bulman, 2020). This led to a challenge by Detention Action (a charity) on the steps the Home Secretary was taking to address the issue of immigration detention in light of the COVID-19 pandemic *(R (on the application of Detention Action) v Secretary of State for the Home Department* [2020.

In this case, an urgent interim relief application was submitted by Detention Action to release 736

---

[1] Senior Law Lecturer at the University of Greenwich, UK; PhD Candidate at Queen Mary University of London, UK; Part-time Law Teacher at the London School of Economics and Political Science, UK.

detainees whose removal was not imminent due to the global pandemic and consequential travel restrictions around the world. The interim application was also lodged on behalf of vulnerable detainees who were medically/physically impaired and those that were 70 years old or above. Detention Action relied on three reports prepared by Professor Coker (a Professor of Public Health) which indicated that 60 percent of the prison and detention population could become infected by COVID-19 rapidly due to overcrowding, poor ventilation and poor hygiene levels. Dr Selina Rajan (a medical doctor) stated that due to the poor healthcare facilities in detention, many detainees could develop pneumonia which may go untreated in detention.

There was a travel ban in place from some 50 countries which meant that the likelihood of removal was no longer reasonably imminent. In the seminal cases of R v Governor of Durham Prison ex parte Hardial Singh [1984] and R (Lumba) v SSHD [2012], it was held that detainees should only be detained for a period that is reasonable in the circumstances.

Mr Justice Swift of the High Court in the present case refused the application for interim relief stipulating that the Home Secretary had taken adequate steps to ensure that detainees could self-isolate effectively in detention (R (on the application of Detention Action) v Secretary of State for the Home Department [2020]. The Court also stated that effective measures were put into place to protect detainees that may be shielding. Nonetheless, around this time there were several stories of detainees living in cramped conditions which contravened the guidance set by Public Health England (Kelly, 2020).

The Court further ruled that even where the country (where the detainee was due to be removed/deported to) had informed the Home Secretary that it was no longer accepting removals, then the Home Secretary was entitled to a short period in which to review the detainee's detention. So, detention can be unlawful if it is not affected within a reasonable timeframe. Guidance for First-tier Tribunal judges (President of the First-tier Tribunal of the Immigration and Asylum Chamber, 2018) stipulates that detention for three months constitutes a substantial period of time and for six months it amounts to a long period of time.

Although, this challenge was dismissed, between 16 March and 21 April 2020, the Home Office released 1000 detainees (Bulman, 2020). The Home Office also confirmed that each case would be considered on its merits, but its priority would be to detain the most serious foreign national offenders (Taylor, 2020). Although, detention was due to be reviewed on a case-by-case basis, detainees that were vulnerable continued to challenge their detention on the premise that it contravened the guidance set out by the Public Health England. In this regard, Bail for Immigration Detainees (a charity that helps detainees) provided legal representation to 109 detainees between 23 March and 30 June 2020, with a success rate of 94 per cent (Bail for Immigration Detainees, 2020). Some even estimate that there were 70 percent fewer migrants held in immigration detention in June 2020 as compared to December 2019 (Waterman, Pillay, Katona, 2021).

Following this case, in the case of R (on the application of Zaly's) v Secretary of State for the Home Department [2020], the claimant challenged the Home Secretary's decision to detain him as he was not only waiting for the outcome of his deportation appeal, but he was unable to be deported to Lithuania in light of the travel restrictions that were in place at that time, making it impossible for the Home Office to remove him within a reasonable timeframe. He also argued that the congregate setting contravened the Public Health England's guidance. His judicial review application was successful, and he was released from detention because of the risks posed to him by his continued detention and the impossibility of his removal.

Alternatives to Detention

The immigration system is deeply flawed because although the detainees were released for a short period of time during the height of the COVID-19 pandemic, they have probably been placed back into detention given that the pandemic is now (slightly) under control; and so, they now face the threat of deportation/removal again. However, making concessions for exceptional circumstances arising from the COVID-19 pandemic allows one to envisage a world where immigration detention may not be necessary. Alternatives to detention should now be given serious consideration. Not only is the immigration detention system deeply flawed, but it is also very costly. According to estimates, immigration detention costs £100 million yearly which equates to approximately £30,000 per detainee (Detention Action, 2021).

Therefore, alternatives to detention should be considered. For example, these include programs that encourage intensive engagement within communities (All Party Parliamentary Group on Migration, 2015). Such measures do not just achieve high compliance rates, but they are also cheaper than the current system (Detention Action, 2022). Detention Action has been running the Community Support Project since 2014 where men who have experienced or are at risk of experiencing long-term detention are looked after. (Detention Action, 2022). Their practical and emotional needs are addressed; they are offered holistic advice and assistance and a plan is created detailing their aims/goals (Detention, Action, 2022). 93 per cent of those that were a part of this programme did not reoffend since joining this project (Detention Action, 2022).

Perhaps instead of detaining individuals, the UK Government could make more widespread use of this program and house those that may have been placed in immigration detention, provide them with medical care as well as other facilities.

What Happened with the Detainees that Remained in Detention?

Finally, it is worth stating that the COVID-19 pandemic had a significant impact on those detainees that remained in detention, as legal visits to detention centres were stopped/restricted. Appointments were being made remotely or by telephone (Independent Monitoring Board, 2021). Bail for Immigration Detainees ceased operating on-site surgeries from March 2020, but it continued to provide a telephonic advice (Independent Monitoring Board, 2021).

It was noted that some solicitors were not returning calls to their clients (Independent Monitoring Board, 2021). There were informal complaints about the telephone connection, both for lawyers and detainees, so detainees found it difficult to maintain access with their solicitors (Independent Monitoring Board, 2021). It was difficult to communicate with detainees as they did not always have access to the internet/mobile phones and so most communication occurred slowly through the postal system (Bail for Immigration Detainees and Medical Justice, 2021). This problem pre-dated the pandemic, but the strict lockdown regimes exacerbated this problem (Bail for Immigration Detainees and Medical Justice, 2021). In several cases, BID was forced to provide representation on receiving partial instructions from detainees, due to the ongoing communication problems (Bail for Immigration Detainees and Medical Justice, 2021).

Conclusion

The UK makes widespread use of immigration detention. This chapter has revealed some of the problems with administrative detention. However, this pandemic showed us that the British State can and should limit the use of administrative detention, as it did during the height of the COVID-19 pandemic.

References

Annual Report of the IMB at Brook House IRC For Reporting Year 1 January – 31 December 2020. (2021). https://s3-eu-west-2.amazonaws.com/imb-prod-storage-1ocod6bqky0vo/uploads/2021/05/Brook-House-AR-2020-for-circulation.pdf

Bulman, M. (2020a, March 22). Woman in yarl's wood tests positive for coronavirus in first confirmed case in uk removal centre. *The Independent*. https://www.independent.co.uk/news/uk/home-news/coronavirus-yarls-wood-immigration-detention-removal-centre-home-office-a9417056.html

Bulman, M. (2020b, May 20). "I Don't Know why I am Still Here": Hundreds Held for Deportation Despite Coronavirus Ban. *The Independent*. https://www.independent.co.uk/news/uk/home-news/coronavirus-travel-ban-uk-detention-deportation-home-office-legal-challenge-a9522811.html

Community Support Project. (2022). Detention Action. https://detentionaction.org.uk/community-support-project/

Detention Action's Briefing on the Nationality and Borders Bill. (2021). chrome-extension://efaidnbmnnnibpcajpcglclefindmkaj/https://detentionaction.org.uk/wp-content/uploads/2021/07/Nationality-and-Borders-Bill-.pdf

Dismantling Detention: International Alternatives to Detaining Immigrants. (2021). https://www.hrw.org/report/2021/11/03/dismantling-detention/international-alternatives-detaining-immigrants

Every day is like Torture: Solitary Confinement and Immigration Detention. (2021). https://hubble-live-assets.s3.amazonaws.com/biduk/redactor2_assets/files/1328/Solitary_Confinement_Report_Final_2.pdf

Guidance on Immigration Bail for Judges of the First-tier Tribunal. (2018). President of the First-tier Tribunal Judge Clements Immigration and Asylum Chamber. chrome-extension://efaidnbmnnnibpcajpcglclefindmkaj/viewer.html?pdfurl=https%3A%2F%2Fwww.judiciary.uk%2Fwp-content%2Fuploads%2F2018%2F05%2Fbail-guidance-2018-final.pdf&clen=786021&chunk=true

Kelly, N. (2020, March 29). We Share Everything": Coronavirus Fears Inside a UK Detention Centre. *The Guardian*. https://www.theguardian.com/uk-news/2020/mar/29/inside-the-detention-centre-where-inmates-fear-coronavirus

R *(on the application of Detention Action) v Secretary of State for the Home Department* [2020] EWHC (UK)

R *(on the application of Zalys) v Secretary of State for the Home Department* [2020] 4 WLUK 86 (UK)

R *v Governor of Durham Prison ex parte Hardial Singh* [1984] 1 WLR 704

R *(Lumba) v SSHD* [2012] AC 245 (UK)

Research Paper: Immigration Bail Hearings during the COVID-19 Pandemic. (2020). chrome-extension://efaidnbmnnnibpcajpcglclefindmkaj/viewer.html?pdfurl=https%3A%2F%2Fhubble-live-assets.s3.amazonaws.com%2Fbiduk%2Fredactor2_assets%2Ffiles%2F1263%2F201214_v6_Immigration_bail_monitoring.pdf&clen=935875&chunk=true

Taylor, D. (2020, March 21). Home Office Released 300 from Detention Centres Amid COVID-19 Pandemic. *The Guardian*. https://www.theguardian.com/uk-news/2020/mar/21/home-office-releases-300-from-detention-centres-amid-covid-19-pandemic

The Report of the Inquiry into the Use of Immigration Detention in the United Kingdom: A Joint Inquiry by the All Party Parliamentary Group on Refugees & the All Party Parliamentary Group on Migration. (2015). https://detention.org.uk/wp-content/uploads/2017/08/immigration-detention-inquiry-report.pdf

Waterman, L., Pillay, M., & Katona, C. (n.d.). The Mass Release of Migrants from UK Immigration Detention During the COVID-19 Pandemic: What can be Learned?. *BJPsych Bulletin*, 1–6. https://doi.org/https://doi.org/10.1192/bjb.2021.110

SHOULD I STAY OR SHOULD I GO: THE PANDEMIC EFFECT ON MIGRATION ASPIRATIONS USING PANEL DATA IN POLAND

Sébastien Michiels[1], David Doyle[2], Evelyn Ersanilli[3], Olga Onuch[4], Gwendolyn Sasse[5], Jacquelin van Stekelenburg[6], and Sorana Toma[7]

Introduction

Has the experience of the COVID-19 pandemic altered migration decision-making and if so, has it dampened or heightened the desire to leave one's home country?

Extant social science proposes two competing hypotheses for us to consider. On the one hand, a public health and economic crisis like the COVID-19 pandemic may have reduced the 'pull' effect of moving abroad. The pandemic further exposed the inequality and precarious situation of migrants in many destination countries including in high income liberal-democracies in western Europe. Highly publicized media reports have shown that migrants were more likely than permanent residents to lose their jobs during lockdowns, see their incomes reduced, and to have experienced worse health outcomes during the pandemic. Furthermore, the temporary closure of many borders, including within the EU (OECD 2020), increased the most basic costs and risks of migration – thus potentially depressing migration intention. On a socio-psychological level, leaving one's family and close friends behind during a deadly health crisis - when return travel is likely to also be restricted – may further discourage individuals' migration aspirations. Again, these factors would reduce the 'pull' of out-migration and raise costs and risks substantially - likely depressing migration intention. Recent research finds indeed a negative impact of the pandemic on migration intentions among Gambians (Bah et al. 2021). The largest declines are found among individuals who were unsure about their intent pre-pandemic and among poorer individuals who are no longer able to afford the costs of migrating.

On the other hand, the pandemic - and its health, political and economic consequences - are likely to also further escalate the pressure of 'push' factors behind out-migration (desire) at home. With the onset of the pandemic, many individuals' economic situation deteriorated and feelings of economic insecurity heightened, as was found in South East Asia (Nakamura and Suzuki 2021) or El Salvador (Durán 2022). As economic factors are some of the main drivers of aspirations to migrate (Onuch et al. 2022), we may also expect an increase in the desire to leave one's country, particularly among those who suffered economic losses due to the pandemic.

These two hypotheses suggest that migration aspirations move in opposite directions, but they may also point to different temporalities of the pandemic effect. Data from El Salvador suggests an initial

[1] Dr. Sébastien Michiels, Centre de Recherche en Economie et Statistique, France. E-mail: sébastien.michiels@ensae.fr
[2] Prof. David Doyle, University of Oxford, UK.
[3] Prof. Evelyn Ersanilli, University of Amsterdam, The Netherlands.
[4] Prof. Olga Onuch, The University of Manchester , UK.
[5] Prof. Gwendolyn Sasse, Zentrum fur Osteuropa und internationale Studien, Germany.
[6] Prof. Jacquelien van Stekelenburg, Vrije Universiteit Amsterdam, The Netherlands.
[7] Prof. Sorana Toma, Ghent University, Belgium.

and temporary deceleration of emigration intentions, followed by a substantial increase in both intentions and actual migrations (Durán 2022). The pandemic is thus likely to have a *differentiated* impact, over time and for different groups, particularly with respect to their economic situation.

Recent research also points to the *moderating role of governments*, or at least of individuals' perception of how state authorities have managed the pandemic and its consequences. Simon et al. (2022) find that Gambians who lost their job during the pandemic are less likely to want to migrate if they trust their government's ability to efficiently manage the post-pandemic recovery.

Research hypotheses

We thus expect a decrease in migration aspirations after the onset of the COVID-19 pandemic (H1). However, we expect this change to be conditioned by individuals' economic situation: those in more constrained material situations, or whose situation worsened, may be more likely to maintain or form new migration aspirations (H2). We further expect this change to be moderated by individuals' levels of trust in their governments: we expect those with a higher level of trust or whose trust increased to be more likely to abandon their migration aspirations and less likely to form new migration aspirations (H3).

Data and Measures

We examine these competing hypotheses by employing original panel data collected by the authors in Poland within the framework of the MOBILISE project (https://mobiliseproject.com/). The survey collects information about residents' attitudes, intentions and experiences of political participation (institutional and non-institutional) and migration, civil society embeddedness and social networks, media consumption, and political attitudes and regime support, along with relevant socio-demographic information.

More specifically, we use two waves of a representative panel survey among Poles collected by a local company (CEBOS) in 2019 (Wave 1 collected between August and September) and 2020-2021 (Wave 2 collected between November and January). The first wave of the surveys were designed to consist of a nationally representative sample (N = 1,500, selected through a stratified, multi-stage, area probability technique) and an additional random sample focused on the five biggest cities in each country (N = 500). All survey interviews were planned to be computer assisted face-to-face interviews. However, due to the pandemic, Wave 2 interviews were switched to telephone mode. Response rates are respectable, at 29% for Wave 1 in Poland, and with an attrition rate of about 25% between the two waves.

Our survey includes a rather classical item to capture **migration aspirations**: "Ideally, if you had the opportunity, would you like to go abroad to live or work some time during the next 2 years, or would you prefer staying in (country of origin)?". For those responding yes, we also collect the destination country they would like to go to.

Results

Table 1 presents some descriptive statistics on the balanced panel sample (i.e., those interviewed at both waves), totaling 1450 individuals. We exclude the 95 cases with missing values on migration aspiration in either 2019 or 2020, so our sample size is made of 1355 individuals.

When we look at the share of those who say they aspire to migrate by wave we see a remarkable stability: 20% in mid-2019 vs. 21% at the end of 2020. But when looking within these groups, we actually see quite a lot of change: some (9.7% of the total sample) who didn't aspire to migrate in 2019 do so in 2020 (we call these recent would-be migrants) and, vice versa, 8.3% aspired to migrate in 2019 but no longer do so at the end of 2020 (no longer would-be migrants). Stable would-be migrants represent, for their part, about 12% of the sample. Thus, among all individuals who expressed an aspiration to migrate at least once, about two thirds have changed their mind within the observation period of the survey.

Table 1. Change in migration aspirations between mid-2019 (Wave 1) and end 2020 (Wave 2)

Migration aspirations 2019	Migration Aspirations 2020		
	No migration aspiration	Migration aspiration	Total
No migration aspiration	947	131	1,078
	70 %	9.7 %	79%
Migration aspiration	109	168	277
	8.3 %	12 %	21%
Total	1,056	299	1,355
	78%	22%	100

Source: MOBILISE Polish Panel Survey (2019-2021)

Given this substantial change in the composition of aspiring migrants, we examine whether and how drivers of migration aspirations changed between the two waves. Adopting a cross-sectional design, we run the same models, using the same set of covariates, in wave 1 (2019) and wave 2 (2020). Figure 1 presents average marginal effects from a series of logistic regression models estimating aspirations to migrate (coded as 0/1) on the balanced sample.

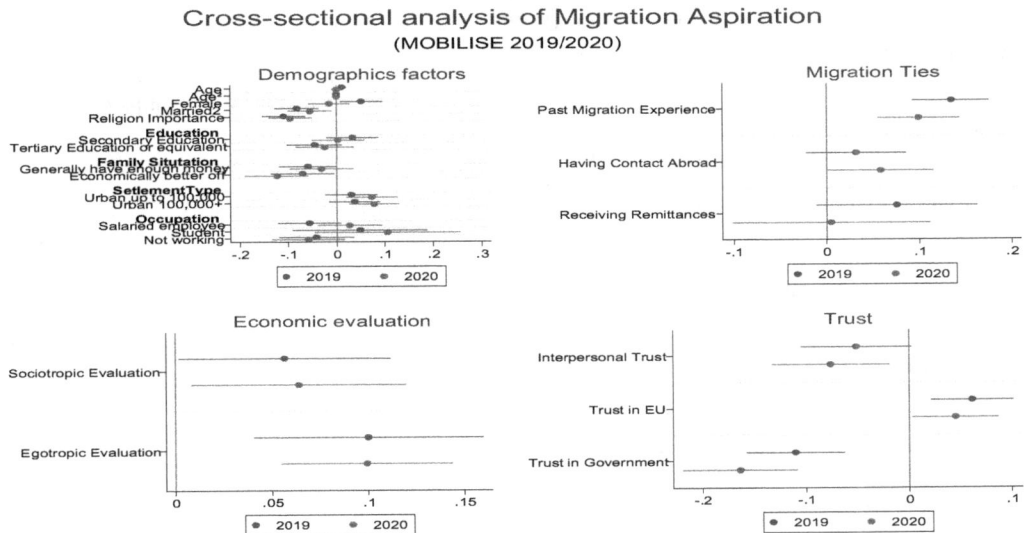

Cross-sectional analysis of Migration Aspiration
(MOBILISE 2019/2020)

Overall we find that drivers of migration are remarkably stable, with a few exceptions. Whereas women were more likely to aspire to migrate in 2019, gender is no longer significantly associated with migration aspirations in 2020. In contrast, whereas residential location was not a driver of aspirations in 2019, living in larger urban settings is positively and significantly associated with the desire to leave one's country. Similarly, having contacts abroad became in 2020 a significant (and positive) driver of migration aspirations.

Individuals whose family financial situation was less good were more likely to wish to leave their country, but similarly so in 2019 and 2020: the difference with the economically better off increased, but not significantly so. Similarly, trusting the national government decreased the likelihood to aspire to migrate, but not significantly more in 2020 than in 2019.

Conclusion

Similar average migration desire across the two waves hides in fact substantial within-individual longitudinal change, in both directions: a sizeable minority formed new migration aspirations between the two waves, while a similarly-sized group gave up their migration plans. However, despite big changes in the composition of those aspiring to migrate, we do not observe much change in drivers of aspirations to migrate pre- and post-pandemic (with the exception of gender, urban setting and prior migration ties). Next to the pandemic, other political changes in Poland during the same period (e.g., the re-election of Duda, political attacks on the judiciary system and on the media, leading, among others to mass-mobilization in October 2020 around changes in abortion law) may have also led certain individuals to form new migration aspirations.

In further research we plan to fully exploit the panel dimension of our data by modelling change in migration aspirations across the two waves, and examining the factors responsible for the different transitions (i.e., maintaining, abandoning or forming new migration aspirations).

References

Bah, T. L., Batista, C., Gubert, F. & McKenzie, D. 2021. "How Has COVID-19 Affected the Intention to Migrate via the Backway to Europe and to a Neighboring African Country? Survey Evidence and a Salience Experiment in The Gambia." Working Paper. Washington, DC: World Bank. https://doi.org/10.1596/1813-9450-9658.

Durán, C. A. 2022. "Intention to Migrate Due to COVID-19: A Study for El Salvador." *Journal of International Migration and Integration*, March. https://doi.org/10.1007/s12134-022-00952-3.

Nakamura, N., and Suzuki, A. 2021. "COVID-19 and the Intentions to Migrate from Developing Countries: Evidence from Online Search Activities in Southeast Asia." *Journal of Asian Economics* 76 (October): 101348. https://doi.org/10.1016/j.asieco.2021.101348.

OECD 2020. "Managing International Migration under COVID-19." https://www.oecd.org/coronavirus/policy-responses/managing-international-migration-under-covid-19-6e914d57/.

Onuch, O., Doyle, D., Ersanilli, E., Sasse G., Van Stekelenburg, J., & Toma, S. 2022. "Protest vs. Migration Intention: Push Factors of Exit & Voice." in. Oslo, Norway.

Simon, M., Schwartz, C., & Hudson, D. 2022. "Covid-19 Insecurities and Migration Aspirations." *International Interactions* 48 (2): 309–26. https://doi.org/10.1080/03050629.2022.1991919.

LEVERAGING OPEN SOURCES TO ESTIMATE MIGRATION MOVEMENTS DURING CRISES

Kirstie Bosman[1], Beth James[2], Rebecca Kitchen[3], and Matt Zelina[4]

Introduction

This paper provides a set of guiding principles for using open sources to estimate the scale of migration movements, specifically to inform time-sensitive policy decisions in contexts of unfolding crises and the COVID-19 pandemic.[5] We focus on movements towards the EU. Our aim is not to uncover the full truth, which would require more robust research, but rather to best approximate, to inform practitioners responding to emergencies under time and intelligence constraints.

This paper is structured as follows. First, we outline data challenges facing migration policymakers responding to crises, including additional challenges posed by the COVID-19 pandemic. Second, we discuss how to leverage open sources to meet those challenges. Third, we present guiding principles to direct such research. Fourth, we demonstrate these with a case study on movements of Afghan nationals towards the EU after the Taliban takeover of Afghanistan. Finally, we summarize our findings and highlight areas for further development.

Data Challenges

Building an accurate understanding of migration movements on the ground requires challenging field work and interviews with stakeholders. Few organisations globally have the resources and will to conduct such research; most are EU or UN agencies. Individual researchers therefore depend heavily on secondary data, which are limited in comparability, recency, and scope. The COVID-19 pandemic heightened these challenges by further restricting the efforts to collect, analyse, and publish data.

Meanwhile, migration practitioners rarely have the luxury of time to build a complete picture of developments, especially when responding to emergencies. The COVID-19 pandemic increased reliance on open sources, as travel to crisis hotspots became not only dangerous, but often impossible. These methods pose formidable challenges, however, as the volume of open information is ever-increasing, and with it risks of misinformation and disinformation.[6]

In these contexts, when reliable information is both most urgently needed and hardest to find, we must develop creative strategies to collect and analyse data.

---

[1] Researcher, Ridgeway Information, UK. E-mail: kirstie.bosman@ridgeway-information.com.
[2] Researcher, Ridgeway Information, UK. E-mail: beth.james@ridgeway-information.com.
[3] Assistant Researcher, Ridgeway Information, UK and Undergraduate Student, University of Kent, UK. E-mail: rak25@kent.ac.uk.
[4] Senior Researcher, Ridgeway Information, UK. E-mail: matt.zelina@ridgeway-information.com.
[5] We define 'open sources' as 'sources that are publicly available'.
[6] We define misinformation as 'misleading information created or disseminated without manipulative or malicious intent' and disinformation as 'deliberate (often orchestrated) attempts to confuse or manipulate people through delivering dishonest information to them' (UNESCO, 2018).

Meeting the Challenges

One way to collect data quickly and remotely is via open sources. This includes large-N data, such as the IOM Displacement Tracking Matrix (dtm.iom.int) and Missing Migrants Project (missingmigrants.iom.int), Eurostat data (2022), and Frontex border crossing data (2022). Other sources include country-specific UNHCR and IOM monitoring, or NGO and other research centers like the Border Violence Monitoring Network (www.borderviolence.eu), the Global Initiative Against Transnational and Organized Crime (globalinitiative.net), and the Mixed Migration Centre (mixedmigration.org). Even less conventional sources, from Alarme Phone Sahara (alarmephonesahara.info/en/) to the Twitter accounts of organisations involved in Mediterranean rescues,[7] can offer valuable insights. Creative and innovative methods can often prove crucial to uncovering new sources.

We can draw limited conclusions from these data points in isolation. Each relies on different methods of operationalization and measurement, making them not directly comparable. Further, open information on politicized issues is often biased, censored, or even deliberately misleading.

To overcome these challenges, researchers can analyse a variety of sources, triangulating and collating them systematically. In Section IV, we present guiding principles for undertaking such analysis.

Guiding Principles

Our guiding principles for data collection and analysis address the practical challenges of how to (1) collect information remotely under time constraints, and (2) assess its veracity.

Data collection

Collecting data on migration movements using open sources requires creative thinking, innovative methods, and systematic gathering. Understanding the factors shaping migratory journeys and routes from existing research offers insights on where to look.

Researchers seeking to forecast migration movements must leverage a range of sources and cannot exclusively rely on arrival data, which is often outdated and excludes those who are undetected, intercepted or pushed back by border forces, go missing, or die. Understanding the scale of interceptions and push-backs is critical for forecasting movements, as many migrants will re-attempt border crossings.

One strategy we employ is to focus on naturally occurring bottlenecks along migratory routes. The two most significant bottlenecks for EU destinations are the Mediterranean Sea and Turkey. Our case study below demonstrates how focusing on Turkey led us to uncover a valuable, unexpected data source.

Analysis

To analyse open sources, researchers must assess a source's *validity* ('the level of confidence that the information that is recorded objectively reflects the reality of what is being measured') and *credibility* ('the likelihood that an additional completely competent and disinterested source would report the same information based on the same event') (Ackerman and Pinson, 2016, p. 620).

To assess validity, we identify and assess the primary source, thereby increasing or decreasing our confidence that the information is valid. The source's claims must then be corroborated and verified through other sources. Sufficient corroboration occurs when information is confirmed by multiple

---

[7] For example: @RescueMed, @seawatch_intl, @alarm_phone, and @openarms_fund.

(ideally primary) sources.

To assess credibility, we examine a source's intrinsic and extrinsic characteristics. Intrinsic refers to surface integrity, assessed by identifying grammatical mistakes, inconsistencies, and sources of bias. Extrinsic refers to whether the author and institution have credible track records. Even if a source fails these two tests, its information could still be valid. Source credibility could be assessed as high, medium, low/untested, or unreliable.

Researchers must periodically review the accuracy of these evaluations, and ensure that their audience is fully aware of the implications for interpreting analysis.

Limitations

Open source research has many limitations (Pastor-Galindo et al., 2020), a complete discussion of which falls outside the scope of this paper. We do not claim that our methods can reveal the full truth. Rather, they enable us to reasonably assess information and sources in resource-poor research conditions.

Case Study

Our case study applies these principles to estimate the movements of Afghan nationals towards the EU following the Taliban takeover of Afghanistan in August 2021. To do this, we built a dataset using Turkish Coast Guard (TCG) operational reports on migrant interceptions, published on their website (en.sg.gov.tr/latest-activities). By systematically collecting these data, we can forecast changes in the scale of migrant movements toward the EU via Turkey.

Our dataset comprises 1,081 interception events from 30 December 2020 to 12 April 2022. Data for 90 variables are recorded, including the date, location, and nationalities of migrants and smugglers intercepted. The data are updated daily, and therefore useful for monitoring movements in real-time.

The TCG data have several limitations. First, they do not contain demographic information such as gender or age. Additionally, the TCG does not specify how it distinguishes 'rescues' from 'apprehensions' (we combine them as 'interceptions') or migrants from smugglers. Finally, the data may double-count individuals intercepted multiple times. These limitations are in addition to the biases of the TCG and Turkey as key actors in global migration politics.

From 30 December 2020 to 12 April 2022, the TCG intercepted 31,736 migrants. The most common nationalities were:

Table 1. Migrant nationalities detected by the TCG.

Nationality	Migrants intercepted	Percentage of total
1. Afghanistan	6,475	20%
2. Syria	4,241	13%
3. Somalia	4,141	13%
4. Palestine	3,977	13%
5. Democratic Republic of the Congo	2,337	7%
6. Eritrea	1,996	6%
7. Yemen	1,808	6%
8. Pakistan	1,347	4%
9. Bangladesh	946	3%
10. Central African Republic	882	3%
Other	3,586	11%

To test the validity of our data for estimating migratory movements, we compared them with Frontex data on irregular border crossings into the EU (Frontex, 2022). Frontex data are disaggregated by nationality and route and updated monthly, making them easily comparable with the TCG data. We only included Frontex data for the Eastern Mediterranean and Western Balkan routes – on which Turkey is a key transit country – to maximize the chance of measuring the same movements. Our comparison spanned January 2021 to March 2022.

From January 2021 to March 2022, Frontex recorded 107,737 irregular EU border crossings along routes via Tukey. The most common nationalities were:

Table 2. Migrant nationalities detected by Frontex.

Nationality	Irregular border crossings	Percentage of total
• Syria	52,167	48%
• Afghanistan	19,910	18%
• Turkey	6,552	6%
• Pakistan	2,974	3%
• Somalia	2,885	3%
• Democratic Republic of the Congo	2,360	2%
• Nigeria	2,313	2%
• Palestine	2,098	2%
• Morocco	1,851	2%
• Tunisia	1,842	2%
Other	12,785	12%

While the numbers of migrants recorded vary considerably between the TCG and Frontex, and between months, they vary in tandem (Fig. 1). This suggests the datasets are measuring similar phenomena, and therefore that the TCG data may be used to predict changes in the magnitude of movements towards the EU.

To further test our hypothesis, we compared the number of the top four nationalities in both datasets (Afghanistan, Syria, Somalia, and Palestine) as a fraction of all migrants recorded each month. Comparing nationalities as proportions mitigated three sources of variation. First, Frontex recorded over three times as many migrants as the TCG, making absolute figures incomparable. Second, the numbers of migrants recorded by the TCG and Frontex vary significantly by month (Fig. 1). Finally, the magnitude of movements towards the EU varies seasonally (Katsiaficas 2016).

Before analyzing the results, it is important to note the potential impact of time lags. It could take months before someone intercepted by the TCG irregularly enters the EU. Therefore, we might expect to observe changes in TCG data earlier than in Frontex data. This could vary by nationality if some are intercepted more often than others.

Regarding Afghan nationals, co-variation was low from January to September 2021 (Fig. 2). However, the August 2021 Frontex spike may have been a delay of the April 2021 TCG spike, suggesting a five-month lag. Co-variation was high with no lag after October 2021. Regarding Syrian nationals, co-variation was relatively high, with a three-month lag (Fig. 3). Regarding Somalian nationals, co-variation was high with no lag, especially after May 2021 (Fig. 4). Regarding Palestinian nationals, co-variation was relatively high with no lag (Fig. 5).

Figure 1. Total migrants recorded, monthly.

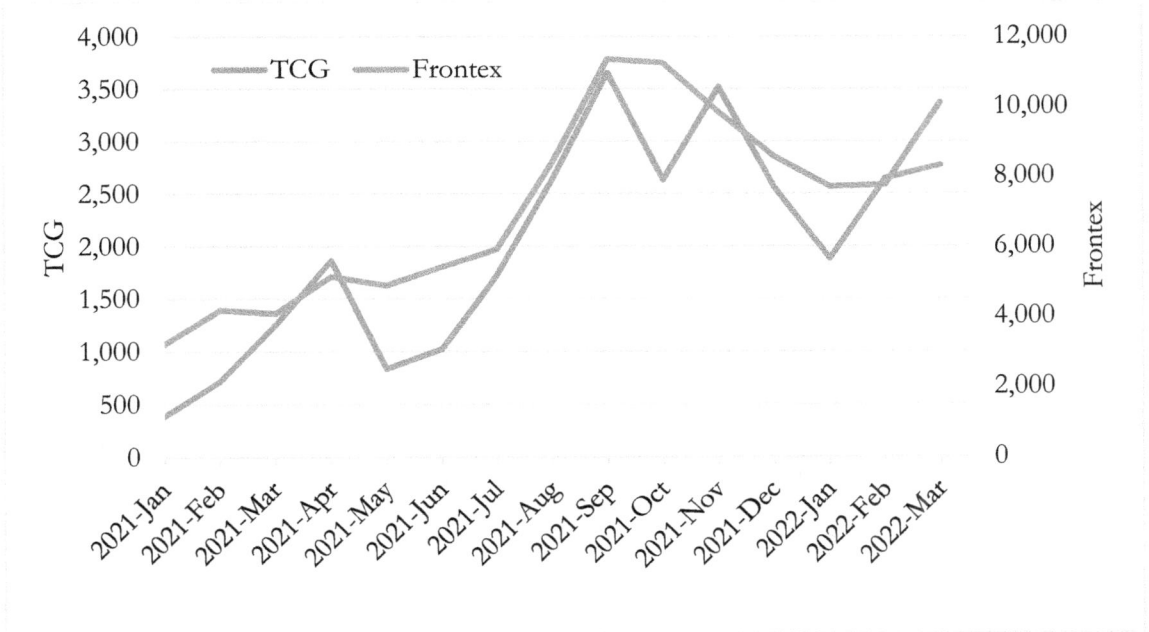

Figure 2. Afghan nationals as a proportion of all migrants detected.

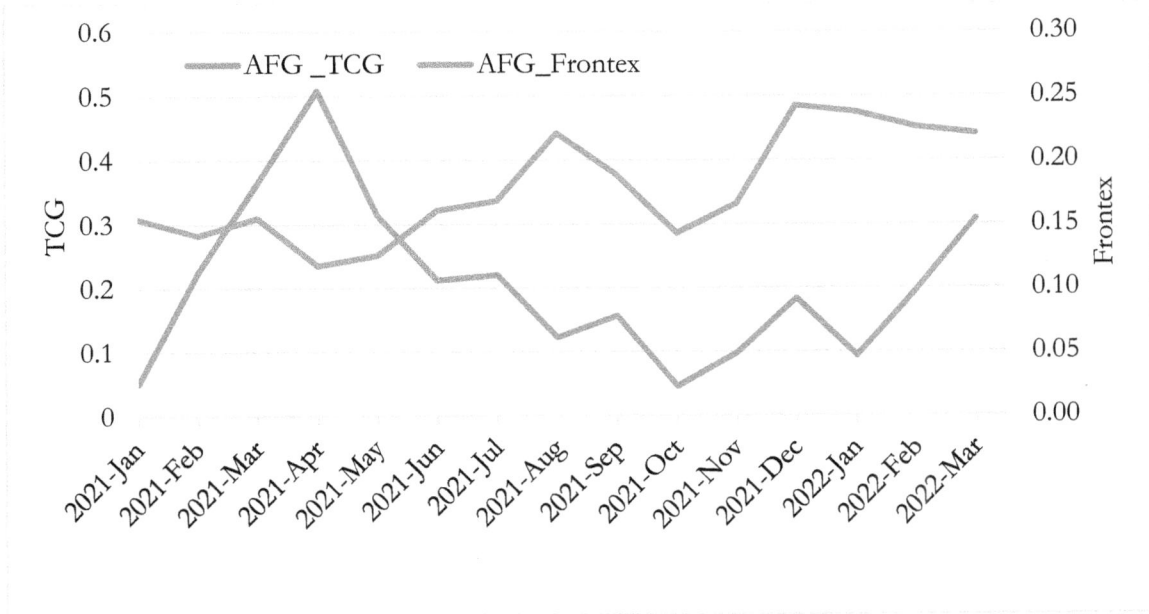

Figure 3. Syrian nationals as a proportion of all migrants detected.

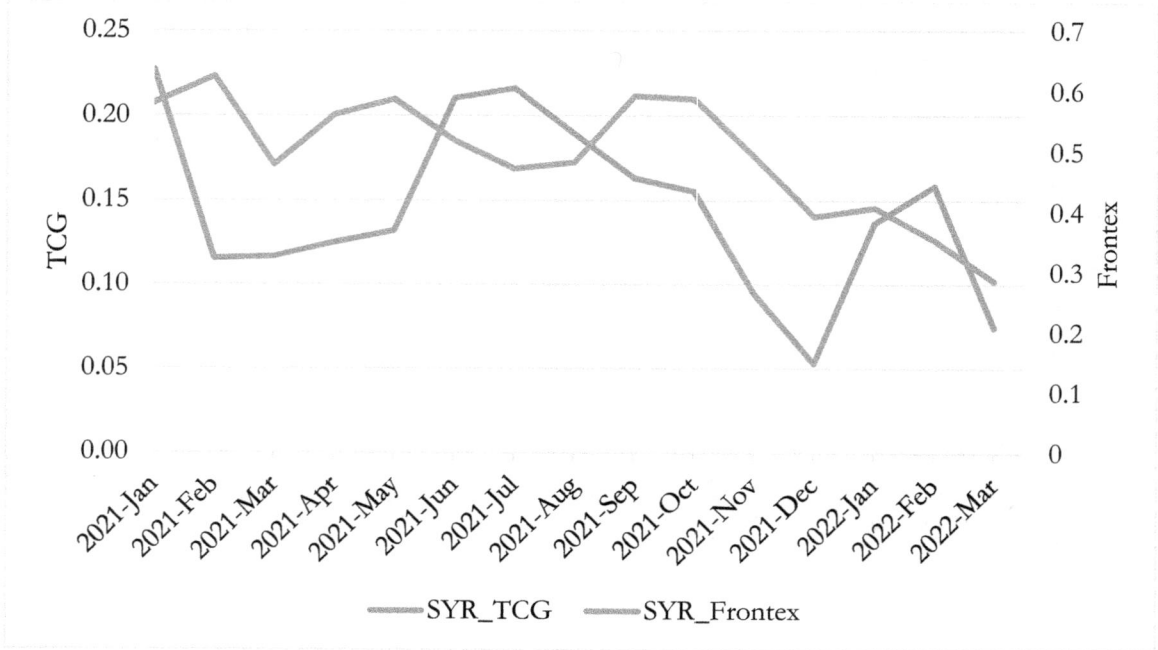

Figure 4. Somalian nationals as a proportion of all migrants detected.

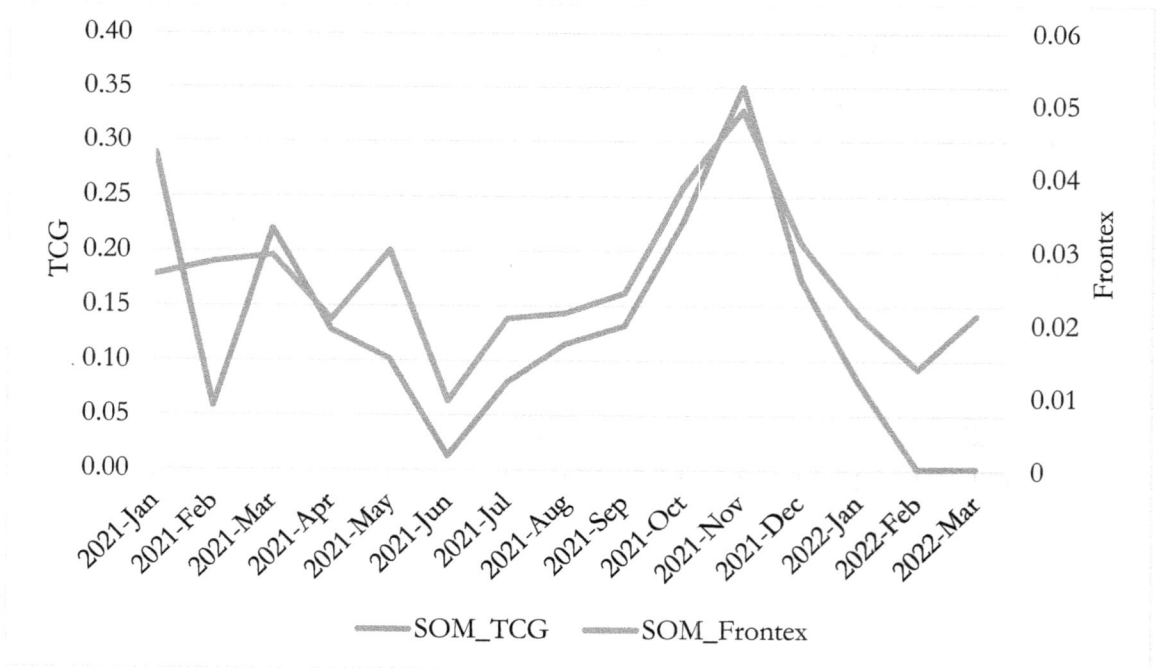

Figure 5. Palestinian nationals as a proportion of all migrants detected.

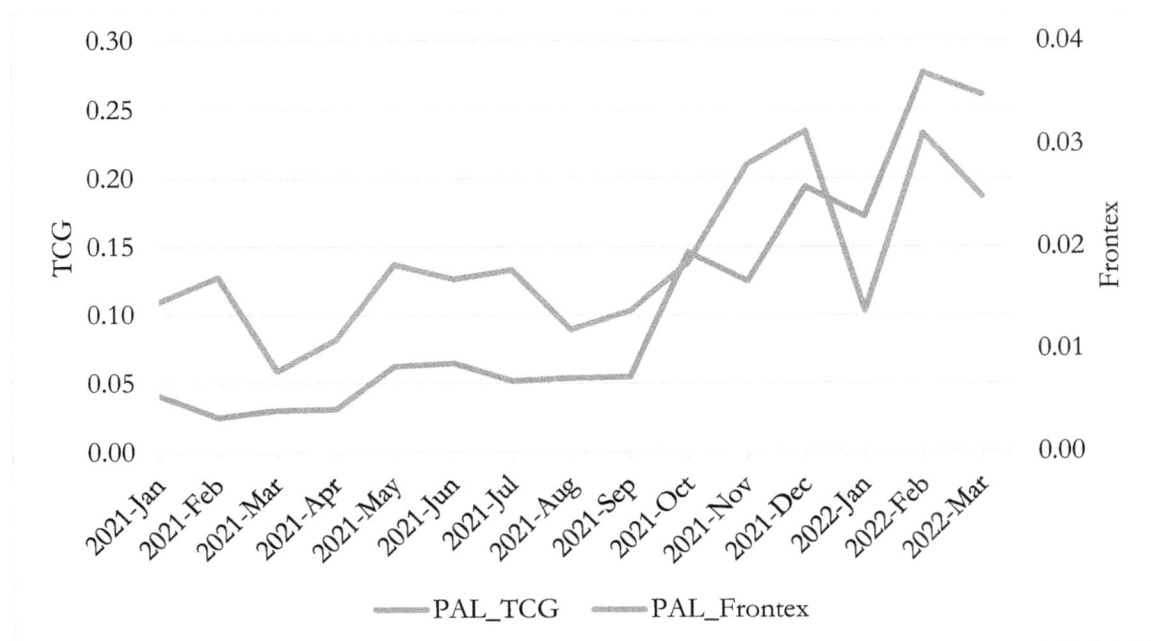

Overall, while preliminary, our results suggest that TCG data strongly predict changes in the magnitude and nationality composition of migratory movements towards the EU.

Conclusion

Leveraging open sources to estimate the scale of migration movements can provide valuable insights to inform time-sensitive policy decisions in imperfect research contexts. However, available open source data may be incomplete, outdated, incomparable, biased, or even misleading. Our TCG case study demonstrates how researchers can mitigate these data challenges by using innovative methods of data collection and validation. There is ample room for further developments, especially on data validation and combining data that are measuring different phenomena. For this case study, further work could include calculating co-variances and the impact of time lags.

References

Ackerman, G. & Pinson, L. (2016). Speaking Truth to Sources: Introducing a Method for the Quantitative Evaluation of Open Sources in Event Data. *Studies in Conflict & Terrorism, 39*(7-8), 617-640. https://doi.org/10.1080/1057610X.2016.1141000

Eurostat (2022). *Asylum applicants by type of applicant, citizenship, age and sex – monthly data (rounded)* [Dataset]. Eurostat. https://ec.europa.eu/eurostat/web/migration-asylum/asylum/database

Frontex (2022). *Detections of illegal border-crossings statistics download (updated monthly)* [Dataset]. Frontex. https://frontex.europa.eu/we-know/migratory-map/

Katsiaficas, C. (2016, June 22). *Asylum Seeker and Migrant Flows in the Mediterranean Adapt Rapidly to Changing Conditions*. Migration Policy Institute. https://www.migrationpolicy.org/article/asylum-seeker-and-migrant-flows-mediterranean-adapt-rapidly-changing-conditions

Pastor-Galindo, J., Nespoli, P., Mármol, F. G., and Pérez, G. M. (2020). The Not Yet Exploited Goldmine of OSINT: Opportunities, Open Challenges and Future Trends. *IEEE Access 8*, 10282-10304. https://ieeexplore.ieee.org/abstract/document/8954668

UN DESA (2019). *International migrant stock 2019* [Dataset]. UN DESA. https://www.un.org/en/development/desa/population/migration/data/index.asp

UNESCO (2018). *Journalism, 'Fake News' & Disinformation*. UNESCO. https://unesdoc.unesco.org/ark:/48223/pf0000265
552

VOLATILE FUTURES: FIRST-GENERATION MIGRANTS' PERCEPTION OF TIME IN A COVID-19 CRISIS

Franka Zlatic[1]

In this paper, I discuss how COVID-19 changed the way first-generation individual migrants in the UK perceive time, but also increasingly uncertain future. Following methodological de-nationalism (Anderson, 2019) and super-diversity (Vertovec, 2007), this research encompasses individual migrants, i.e. those who have moved alone, of various national and ethnic origins and follows their settlement in the UK. This work is part of my doctoral project at the University of Nottingham and methods used were semi-structured interviews, participant observation, photo-elicitation method, and counter-mapping.

Time

"Time is a challenging concept. The term means both too much and too little and is simultaneously overanalysed and taken for granted" (Griffiths, 2014:1992). In terms of migration, there is an overarching question of the past (where migrants come from), the present (where they are now) and the future (where they see themselves). In the case of first-generation individual migrants, their transnational lives and 'feet in both worlds', practically mean continuous visits to the past (through circular migration and visits to their home country), coming back to the present (host country) and rethinking the future as "[t]hese all point to complex and contradictory relationships between the past, present and future, which are likely to exist in tension simultaneously for individuals." (Griffiths et al., 2013:np).

While the concept of time has been present in migration related research for a while now, most time related research on migration concerns legal status of migrants, whereas this work considers the concept of time from a personal and emotional perspective. The life-course perspective as it is sometimes called, "is the passage of time, marked personally and collectively. It is thereby intimately related to subjectivity" (Griffiths et al., 2013:np). Being therefore implemented mostly within the context of irregular migration, or in terms of the length of legal permitted stay, the concept of time seems to escape the ones that have actually settled in the host country.

In this work, time is anything but linear and as Gray (2011) argues, often in disharmony with hegemonic clock time. Various experiences with time and different scales of time "such as natural and cultural times, time in relation to life-course and employment, or social time versus bureaucratic or industrial times" (Hughes, 2022:194) can stand in tension with one another, especially in the case of young people (Furlong and Cartmel, 1997) such is the case with this research. Robertson's (2014) use of the concept of "'staggered' migration pathways in itself marks an important intervention in questioning the linearity and unidirectionality of migration pathways" (Baas and Yeoh, 2019:165).

When it comes to first-generation individual migrants, their transnational lives enable them to visit

---

[1] PhD researchers, University of Nottingham, UK. E-mail: Franka.Zlatic@nottingham.ac.uk

recollections of their past and present while constantly thinking about the future as well. Frequent visits to their home countries often mean 'going back' both spatially and temporally, which affirm the non-linear perception of time within their transnational practices. In addition, the use of technology and being virtually present in several places at once brings the discussion even further as adding temporality into the picture, or "global synchronisation of time" as Griffiths et al. (2013) call it, makes the migrants wish they can live in two places physically as well (Baas and Yeoh, 2019:163).

When it comes to future, while for many of us it is a new feeling to negotiate, "there are many in our society for whom such uncertainty has been a familiar companion for some time" (Hughes, 2017:np). The concept of future in first-generation migrants' lives is not only distant but often abstract and highly volatile. The presence of COVID-19 increased the feelings of uncertainty when it comes to future plans, and it also in some cases for the first time, introduced the idea of return migration. In that way, time becomes "cyclical in that it folds the future into the present. It is not simply that we are 'made' by our pasts, but that 'humans as cultural and social beings are future oriented' (Adam, 2004 in Griffiths et al., 2013:np).

While being uncertain, futures are also often postponed and sometimes described as 'not yet' futures, where future is not a "homogenous period but can be split in various ways, including between the near future and a longer-term horizon" (Guyer, 2007 in Griffiths et al., 2013). Furthermore, during this time of increased global uncertainty, migrants have started to question their life decisions and readjust their priorities. Interestingly, while future in the host country is uncertain, most of individual migrants are certain they would have no future if they remained in their home countries in the first place (Griffiths et al., 2013).

Volatile Futures

Methodology

Even though being seemingly heterogenous and diverse, one of the things that migrants in my PhD research have in common is that most of them face uncertainty when it comes to their plans for the future. From December 2020 until September 2021, I have conducted 27 online semi-structured interviews with participants of various nationalities, both EU and non-EU. Nineteen participants were female, eight were male and participants were between 21 and 36 years old at the time of the interview. Their identities were anonymised and names used are pseudonyms. In addition to semi-structured interviews, and as was said at the very beginning, I utilised two visual methods as well: photo elicitation method and a counter-mapping method (Zlatic, 2021), along with the participant observation. However, data included into this paper reflects data gathered from interviews only and the participants I interviewed "do not reflect the totality of the temporal experience of immigrants, since immigrants are also ordinary people whose experience in many respects does not differ from that of 'native' residents. But in several other respects their experience does differ, and it is those fault lines, in which new temporalities are inscribed, that I set out to describe" (Cwerner, 2001:18).

Findings

The messy reality of life, that was previously mentioned as well, "means that moments of time cannot be taken out of context and nor can they be reduced to the two-dimensional world of movement forwards or backwards" (Griffiths et al., 2013). In that way, migrants often talk about their 'old friends', 'old life' or speak about 'back home' which brings the complexity between spatial and temporal dimensions to the front as the terminology does not reflect age of those people and friends, but their temporal positionality in migrants' lives. In that sense, going 'back' home, or visiting home country feels like going backwards symbolically as well and one should only go forward:

> "This is a question that to be honest, is going through my mind all the time, because I feel like, on the realistic point of view, it doesn't have to mean that I'm taking a step back just because I'm going back to Portugal, but I have the feeling that in my point of view I guess that I would kind of feel that way." - Miguel

When it comes to going 'back', "the paradox between the migrants' will to return and the forever delayed return creates a particular problem and exercises a direct influence on their time perspective" (Elchardus et al. 1987: 146). The migrants' attitudes to their homeland may be deeply affected by their economic and social achievements in the host society. The issue of "return (projected, planned, desired, postponed or impossible) thus plays a fundamental role in the migrants' temporal experience" (Cwerner, 2001:12). In many cases, it was career prospects that kept migrants in the host country, while they started thinking about return migration at the same time due to recently questioned priorities, as told by Androula:

> "Makes me really sad, but at the same time I know that it's not enough of a reason for me to go back. Like I don't know, if something happened to my parents then maybe I would consider going back or something but thinking about these things, about the future makes me really sad, but I know that I have to be abroad because I still need to sort out my career and what I'm going to do before I even consider going back because there's not very many career options for me."

Individual migrants are in such cases torn between wanting a better future for themselves and their careers and feeling responsibility to provide and care for their families and to be physically close to their 'old' lives. In case of Eleni, a female migrant from Cyprus, even though she is aware of how important career is in the case of young people, she admits how COVID has changed her perspective:

> "It made me think of the important things in life, what is important for me to continue in the UK, you know from moneywise to knowledge wise and skills wise. In regard to my family as well, I think COVID has put that perspective for me [...], What if something happened to my parents, what would I do in that situation? What would I do if my family was not well? And I was just thinking maybe I can develop things in Cyprus, and be with my family which is important to me and actually contribute in my field of work and develop it."

COVID was the main reason why Maria, a twice migrant who moved from Romania to Spain, and then to the UK, started thinking about long-term future and the way she feels in the UK during a crisis:

> "Right now, I feel like I've never really felt like I wanted to stay there forever. And with this COVID situation it's made it even harder to picture yourself living in a country where you don't really know anyone. So, I think the answer would be no – right now I don't see myself living in the UK for the rest of my life, I think it's more of a temporary thing for me."

Such decisions are often perceived in a form of postponed temporalities. Migrants know their parents and grandparents are getting older, but it is still difficult to decide to permanently return. Some of them are waiting for 'things to change' and in the meantime, they are unable to plan or to action on their hopes and fears. In that sense, those migrants remain in-between and temporally liminal:

> "I thought I won't stay here, stay down here and but some many things happened in the past year now and then because I'm the only child I don't have any siblings and now I see my parents getting old and I just feel I can't leave them alone in China

anymore. I just started to think I may move back to China in future. Eventually. But I didn't make my mind yet." – Xiuying

As was previously mentioned that simultaneous presence of both host and home countries makes migrants feel they want to be in both places physically as well, the question of future bring some very difficult decisions, which is highlighted, as in the previous case of Xiuying, within migrants who are a single-child:

> "I'm just scared of that thing when my parents grow old that I have no brothers or sisters and siblings to take care of them. So, in that case I will need to be in two places at once, which will be very difficult." – Lena

In some cases and within some migrants, time is perceived as a "resource, a commodity that one can have too much or too little of" (Griffiths, 2014:2003). In that sense migrants whose parents are older, or who still have grandparents, fear they will 'run out of time' and experience feelings of responsibility, guilt and time that is pressuring them to make decisions sooner later than later especially during COVID times:

> "A few months ago, I did consider going back home. But not because I didn't feel at ease in the UK but because I thought you know my time had come simply to go back to my family. My family situation is, I mean for everyone who is in their 30s or 40s, it's just really hard to be away from your parents when you know that they are ageing and that you will run out of time at some point and that you will not get to enjoy those moments with your parents" - Mariana

Preliminary findings suggest it is rarely possible to talk about linear construction of time in migration related research, but also it is equally difficult to talk about plans and projections for the future. With the introduction of COVID-19, first-generation individual migrants started to think about their options more frequently and it made them question their priorities. Many of them started to think about returning to their home countries, however, such decisions are seldom easy and straightforward, and therefore remain a not-yet future. COVID-19 induced crisis can be said to have compressed the time migrants have as it put pressure on them to make decisions sooner than they have anticipated.

References

Anderson, B. (2019). "New directions in migration studies: towards methodological de-nationalism." Comparative Migration Studies 7(1): 36.

Baas, M. and B. S. A. Yeoh (2018). "Introduction: Migration studies and critical temporalities." Current Sociology 67(2): 161-168.

Cwerner, S. B. (2001). "The Times of Migration." Journal of Ethnic and Migration Studies 27(1): 7-36.

Elchardus M, I. Glorieux, M. Scheys (1987) Time, cultures, and coexistence. Studi Emigrazione: International Journal of Migration Studies. (86):138-154.

Furlong, A. and F. Cartmel (1997). Young People and Social Change: Individualization and Risk in Late Modernity, Open University Press.

Gray, B. (2011). "Becoming non-Migrant: Lives Worth Waiting for." Gender, Place & Culture 18 (3): 417–432

Griffiths, M., et al. (2013). Migration, Time and Temporalities: Review and Prospect. COMPAS Research Resources Paper. Oxford.

Griffiths, M. (2014). "Out of Time: The Temporal Uncertainties of Refused Asylum Seekers and Immigration Detainees." Journal of Ethnic and Migration Studies 40(12): 1991-2009.

Hughes, V. (2022). "Tense times for young migrants: temporality, life-course and immigration status." Journal of Ethnic and Migration Studies 48(1): 192-208.

Hughes, V. (2017) Uncertainty: how to imagine a future while living in Limbo?. Social Science Space https://www.socialsciencespace.com/2017/04/making-sense-society-vanessa-hughes/. Accessed 26 April 2022

Robertson, S. (2018). "Migrant, interrupted: The temporalities of 'staggered' migration from Asia to Australia." Current Sociology 67(2): 169-185.

Vertovec, S. (2007). "Super-diversity and its implications." Ethnic and Racial Studies 30(6): 1024-1054.

Zlatic, F. (2021, December 14). Visualising the Voice: How counter-mapping gives authority back to research participants [Online]. The Sociological Review Magazine. https://doi.org/10.51428/tsr.vgyt1385